THE BIG 50

CHICAGO CUBS

The Men and Moments That Made the Chicago Cubs

Carrie Muskat

TRIUMPH
B O O K S

Library of Congress Cataloging-in-Publication Data

Names: Muskat, Carrie, author.
Title: The big 50 Chicago Cubs : the men and moments that made the Chicago Cubs / Carrie Muskat.
Description: Chicago, Illinois : Triumph Books, [2020] |
Identifiers: LCCN 2020058515 | ISBN 9781629377483 (paperback) | ISBN 9781641255899 (epub)
Subjects: LCSH: Chicago Cubs (Baseball team)—History.
Classification: LCC GV875.C6 M87 2020 | DDC 796.357/640977311—dc23
LC record available at https://lccn.loc.gov/2020058515

This book is available in quantity at special discounts for your group or organization. For further information, contact:

Triumph Books LLC
814 North Franklin Street
Chicago, Illinois 60610
(312) 337-0747
www.triumphbooks.com

Printed in U.S.A.
ISBN: 978-1-62937-748-3

Design by Andy Hansen
Page production by Patricia Frey
All photos courtesy of AP Images unless otherwise indicated.

For Cubs fans

[Contents]

[Foreword]

The 2015 Cubs season was a dream season. We turned things around and won a wild-card spot; beat the Pirates, then the Cardinals; and got to the NLCS—and then had our hearts just shattered when we were swept by the New York Mets.

In 2016, we put it all together and finished what we thought we were going to do in '15. From start to finish in '16, we were the best team and finished it off with that epic Game 7, which was the icing on top of a season that will never be forgotten in baseball history.

There was a lot of nervous energy before the last out in Game 7. I was thinking, *Don't drop the ball, follow it all the way in*—all the basic things. I was a little nervous with the play, because I thought the runner was a little faster and it was a little wet because of the rain and Kris [Bryant] was coming in. Once you catch it and hands go up, it's party time.

I did put the ball in my back pocket. That was predetermined with the division series and the championship series too. I still have the championship series ball. That's history. We were on the right side of history, and it can never be taken from us.

My first year with the Cubs, in 2012, we lost 101 games. I've seen the whole organization transform from then to making things happen right away. The change was from top to bottom and included everyone who worked here, from the clubhouse staff to the players. It was the whole organization, and not just the baseball operations, but the business side and everyone. It was cool to see that grow.

As the years went on—2012, '13, '14—the front office traded players as part of the rebuilding process, and it was really tough to have guys dealt midseason because that's who you go to spring training with and who you go to battle with every day. After 2014, when the Cubs traded

Jeff Samardzija, it felt like this would be the last time they'd be trading guys. And then in 2016, we celebrated with a World Series championship.

When we won in '16, I thought about past Cubs players. Ernie Banks—when he was around I got to know him well and it was really cool to talk to him about the game. Billy Williams, Rick Sutcliffe, Ryne Sandberg, Ryan Dempster, Kerry Wood—so many people have put this uniform on. And there are so many great Cubs players who never got to hold that trophy.

After being part of that incredible season, I'm looking forward to reading more about Cubs history in this book.

It's different when you wear this Cubs uniform. That 2016 team was a feel-good team and made everyone who ever played here feel good too. Winning the World Series was something that everyone who has ever put this uniform on could be proud of.

Anthony Rizzo is a first baseman for the Chicago Cubs and a three-time All-Star. In 2016, he helped the Cubs win their first World Series title since 1908.

THE BIG 50

CHICAGO CUBS

1

GAME 7, 2016 WORLD SERIES

The morning of November 2, 2016, began like any other day on the road for Chicago Cubs pitcher Kyle Hendricks, who was with his fiancé, Emma. They had breakfast near the team hotel in Cleveland, then lounged around before it was time to prepare for that night's game.

"When I left the hotel to go to the park, I kind of gave Emma a little look—*I'm pitching Game 7*," Hendricks said. "But it really was no different—it was strange. I think it goes back to the mental space I was in at the time was so simplified and focused on execution. It was a normal day."

It was anything but a normal day for generations of Cubs fans. Their beloved team was one win away from its first World Series championship since 1908. The Cubs had overcome a 3–1 deficit in this series and could end decades of angst and frustration by winning Game 7 that night against the Indians at Progressive Field.

In 2015, manager Joe Maddon's first year with the team, the Cubs won 97 games and reached the postseason as a wild-card team. He had dismissed any talk that the Cubs were "cursed."

"I've never really dealt with the word *curse*—I don't believe in those kind of things," Maddon said. "As a team, my expectations are to get to the playoffs, win the division, and then play the last game of the year and win it. That's the expectation of all of us."

But that first season ended with a loss to the New York Mets in the National League Championship Series. The Cubs began the 2016 season with nearly the same roster but were missing leadoff man Dexter Fowler, a free agent who was rumored to be headed to the Orioles after signing a three-year deal.

"[Anthony Rizzo] told me, 'Good luck, I'm going to miss you, my man,'" said Fowler, who had a little surprise for his Cubs teammates.

On February 25, before spring training games began, Maddon gathered the players on a backfield at their complex in Mesa, Arizona. He said he had a special announcement and stood on the mound, hoping everyone was paying attention to him. Fowler snuck up behind the players, having decided to sign a one-year, $8 million deal.

The main motivation? Fowler said they had some unfinished business after reaching the NL Championship Series in 2015.

"My heart's here," Fowler said of the Cubs.

Their leadoff man was back.

In June, Wilson Contreras was promoted from Triple-A Iowa and delivered a pinch-hit two-run homer in his first at-bat. The Cubs had improved their catcher situation.

Third baseman Kris Bryant became a leading Most Valuable Player candidate on June 27 when he hit three home runs and two doubles in Cincinnati. Bryant, who finished with six RBIs, also played three positions in the game, moving from third base to right field to left field.

The kids could play.

The Cubs had a seven-game lead at the All-Star break and filled another gap at the trade deadline when they acquired controversial closer Aroldis Chapman from the New York Yankees. The left-hander, whose fastball regularly registered at 100 mph, had begun that season serving a 30-game suspension for violating Major League Baseball's domestic violence policy. Cubs executives made certain Chapman understood their own expectations before the deal was finalized.

"You can't take for granted the position we're in right now," Cubs president of baseball operations at the time, Theo Epstein, said. "We believe in these guys. We feel like we have a chance to do something special, but there's a lot of work ahead."

The Cubs did have a special season, leading MLB with 103 wins. They ousted the San Francisco Giants in the NL Division Series and rallied against the West Division champion Los Angeles Dodgers in the Championship Series, including a win over Clayton Kershaw in Game 6 to advance.

Epstein and then-general manager Jed Hoyer had helped end the Boston Red Sox's long World Series drought in 2004, but the rebuilding process with the Cubs had been far more extensive. They lost 101 games in their first season in Chicago in 2012.

"This is more special," Hoyer said of the 2016 Cubs. "To come in here and do this in year five with all these kids, it really is special. With anything in life, if something is difficult and you have some adversity, it is sweeter."

Maddon liked to say he wasn't superstitious, just a little "'stitious." He tucked his late father's Anaheim Angels cap from the 2002 World Series in his backpack for support.

The Cubs needed help from above. They fell behind 3–1 in the best-of-seven series against the Indians, then won Game 5 at Wrigley Field on October 30. Two days later, 22-year-old shortstop Addison Russell smacked a grand slam and finished with six RBIs to spark a 9–3 win and even the series.

It was 69 degrees and cloudy for Game 7 in Cleveland with a slight chance of rain in the forecast. Fowler—whom Maddon pumped up every at-bat by saying, "You go, we go"—got everyone in the ballpark going with a leadoff home run off ace Corey Kluber. The Indians tied it in the third, but the Cubs answered with two more runs in the fourth. Javier Baez led off the fifth with another homer off Kluber, and Anthony Rizzo added an RBI single.

Time to start the party in Wrigleyville? Not yet.

Hendricks was lifted in the fifth after a two-out walk to Carlos Santana and was replaced by veteran Jon Lester.

"When I came out of the game, that's when all the emotions started flooding, and maybe that was because I didn't have anything in my control," Hendricks said. "It almost took me back to being a fan again when you're growing up as a kid, watching your favorite teams play in the World Series, how nervous and anxious you are. That's how I became, watching the end of the game there. I loved every second of it."

David Ross, who had announced he was retiring after the season, entered with Lester, who was greeted with a single by Jason Kipnis. But Kipnis reached second on a bad throw by Ross. When the 39-year-old catcher couldn't handle a Lester pitch to Francisco Lindor, Santana and Kipnis scored.

Ross, dubbed "Grandpa Rossy" by the young Cubs, partially made up for his miscue in the sixth with a home run off one of Cleveland's toughest relievers, Andrew Miller. The Cubs led 6–3.

The Indians didn't go away.

In the Cleveland eighth, the Tribe had a runner on and two outs when Lester gave way to Chapman, whom Maddon wanted to get the final four

Ben Zobrist's go-ahead RBI double in the 10th inning of Game 7 propelled the Cubs to victory in the 2016 World Series and earned him MVP honors.

outs. But the Indians weren't intimidated by the lefty's fastballs. Brandon Guyer greeted Chapman with an RBI double, and Rajai Davis followed with a two-run homer off a fastball. NBA star LeBron James led the cheering Indians fans at Progressive Field. The Cubs fans in the crowd of 38,104—and there were many—groaned. The game was tied at 6.

Chapman retired the side in order in the Indians ninth, and then nature intervened. Rain prompted the umpires to call for the tarp and halted play before the 10th. The 17-minute delay gave Cubs fans a chance to breathe—and Jason Heyward time to regroup his teammates. The outfielder walked through the visitors' clubhouse and tapped players on the shoulders.

"Weight room—now," he said. The players squeezed into the cramped space.

The 2016 season was the first of an eight-year contract for Heyward, but he had not lived up to the hype, batting a feeble .230. Early in his career with the Braves, he'd been mentored by players such as Ross, Chipper Jones, Brian McCann, and Tim Hudson.

Heyward's message in the weight room?

"He said, 'We're the best team in baseball for a reason,'" Ross said. "He said, 'These are your brothers here. Fight for your brothers and just stay positive.'"

Epstein was on his way to talk to officials about the delay when he saw the players huddled together. He left them alone. Chapman was in tears. The Cubs' theme in 2016 was, "We never quit." They were reminded of that during the brief but critical meeting.

"Nobody can take this away from us," first baseman Anthony Rizzo said. "We have each other."

Kyle Schwarber added, "We win this right here."

The heartbeat of the Cubs was strong. Schwarber symbolized that. He had suffered a knee injury in the third game of the year that knocked him out of the regular season but miraculously healed well enough to get the OK to bat in the World Series. Designated hitter was the perfect assignment for Schwarber, who singled to open the 10th when play resumed and was lifted for pinch-runner Albert Almora Jr.

Bryant then flied out, but Almora, in a heads-up move, advanced on the play. Rizzo was intentionally walked to set up Ben Zobrist, and Zobrist lined an RBI double down the left-field line past diving third baseman Jose Ramirez. Almora scored, and Zobrist leaped at second base, punching his fist in the air. Miguel Montero added an important RBI single for an 8–6 lead.

Cubs fans were weary of hearing "wait until next year" so many times—could this be it?

The Indians, whose fan base had not celebrated a championship since 1948, added to the drama. Davis hit an RBI single with two outs in the Cleveland 10th off Carl Edwards Jr. Maddon had asked Mike Montgomery to warm up several times during the game and with Davis— the potential tying run—at first, finally called on him. On his second pitch, Montgomery got Michael Martinez to ground out, Bryant-to-Rizzo. The Cubs won 8–7, and it was time to party.

The longest championship drought in professional sports was over.

As the trophy was formally presented to Cubs owner Tom Ricketts and Epstein in the locker room, the players were splashing each other with champagne and beer and chanting, "We never quit, we never quit." Former players Kerry Wood, Ryne Sandberg, Ryan Dempster, and Billy Williams joined in the revelry—while, for others in the room, thoughts drifted to iconic Cubs like Ernie Banks and Ron Santo—both gone now— and so many more who had never even reached a postseason.

"I think the rain delay was the best thing that ever happened to us, to be honest," Hoyer said. "Maybe after 108 years, you get some divine intervention?"

When the Cubs returned to Chicago the next morning, the team bus passed a cemetery. Cubs hats and pennants were draped over some of the tombstones. The bricks of Wrigley Field's outer walls were covered in multicolored messages, written in chalk, many of them love notes to family members and friends who had died without seeing their favorite team win a World Series.

Lester heard from a fan who had taken a radio to his father's gravesite so they could listen to the games together.

"That resonated pretty hard for me," Lester said. "That was a pretty cool moment that these fans shared with their family members, that they've had so many years of heartache—and we were able to give them the championship that this city deserves."

2

MR. CUB

If you had the good fortune to meet Ernie Banks, he probably asked how you were doing. He would've flashed his cherubic grin and inquired about your husband or wife. Maybe you got lucky, as I did in July 2001 when my husband and I bumped into Mr. Cub in a Cooperstown, New York, shop during Hall of Fame induction weekend, and he broke into song. Ernie Banks was in perfect voice.

The sun'll come out
Tomorrow
So ya gotta hang on
'Til tomorrow
Come what may
Tomorrow, tomorrow!
I love ya tomorrow!
You're always
A day
Away!

It was an appropriate song for the cheery Banks, who played 19 seasons with the Cubs, winning the National League's Most Valuable Player award in back-to-back seasons, 1958 and '59.

"Ernie was always an optimistic-type guy," teammate Fergie Jenkins told me. "He was always upbeat, never talked about himself. It was always about the team, what we should be doing."

Banks learned from some of the best players in the Negro Leagues. When he was 19 years old, he played for the Kansas City Monarchs with superstars Satchel Paige, Josh Gibson, and Elston Howard. The Cubs signed the slender shortstop on September 8, 1953, and he made his major league debut nine days later.

The Cubs had signed infielder Gene Baker in 1950, but his big-league debut was delayed until the team added Banks. Writer Wendell Smith quoted Wid Matthews, the Cubs' director of player personnel, as saying the team didn't think Baker was ready. However, his arrival most likely was stalled because the Cubs didn't have another African American player until they signed Banks. For a variety of reasons (one of them, pairing roommates in those days), having two Black players would make travel easier than if they only had one.

Banks and Baker arrived at Wrigley Field on the same day, September 14, 1953. Banks was 22 and came from the Monarchs, where he had hit .380 with 23 homers. Baker, a relative veteran after four solid seasons with Los Angeles in the Pacific Coast League, was six years older. The Cubs were playing host that day to the Brooklyn Dodgers and Jackie Robinson, the first player to break the color barrier in the major leagues.

"First time I walked on the field, [Robinson] came across over to third base, and he said, 'I'm glad to see you here, and I know you can make it,'" Banks told me. "'You've got a lot of ability. Just listen.' And that's what I did."

After one game, Baker told Banks that his Cubs teammates were mad at the shortstop. Why?

"He said, 'You're hustling too much, you're showing everybody up,'" Banks said. "I said, 'I thought you're supposed to play hard. What should I do?' He said, 'Keep on doing it.' He was a very bright guy. He was the brightest guy I've ever been around. He allowed me to learn from my own experiences."

Baseball came easy to Banks, whose powerful wrists helped him set a single-season record for shortstops with 44 home runs in 1955. He led the major leagues in homers and RBIs in 1958 with 47 and 129, respectively, and belted 45 and paced all of baseball with 143 RBIs the next year.

His knees forced him to switch from shortstop to first base in 1962—and Banks had to make another adjustment when Leo Durocher was named manager in 1966. The fiery Durocher acknowledged that Banks "was a great player in his time. Unfortunately, his time wasn't my time."

What was Banks' take on Durocher?

"He brought the energy to the organization in many ways, by excitement and creativity and fear," Banks told me. "Most people kind of belabor the fact that he didn't like me or I didn't like him. It's a normal thing—I've learned this from my own family, and I come from a family of 12—it's a normal thing to kind of create discord between people. But I never allowed it because I learned many years ago that whoever was the boss is in charge and I respected that.

"Most people thought Leo didn't like me and I didn't like him," Banks said. "I never met a person I disliked. That's my philosophy."

Which is what made Banks so endearing.

His power numbers dropped after he hit 37 homers in 1962; from that year until his retirement following the 1971 season, he only hit more than 30 home runs once (32, in 1968). But Banks did reach the 500 home run milestone on May 12, 1970, connecting against Atlanta's Pat Jarvis in front of a sparse crowd of 5,264 at Wrigley Field.

He and contemporaries Willie Mays, Mickey Mantle, and Eddie Mathews, all members of the 500 club, were born in the same year, 1931—yet Mays, Mantle, and Mathews had the one thing Banks never got: the chance to play in a World Series.

Banks still maintained his enthusiasm.

"He's an inspiration to the older guys as well as the rookies," pitcher Phil Regan said on the day Banks hit his 500th. "Sometimes we complain about the travel or the conditions or something, and then we see Ernie lifting everybody up. All he wants to do is go out there and play ball."

Durocher showed his respect for Banks at the end of the 1971 season. Banks was batting a feeble .181, but Durocher started him for the final three home games against the Phillies, knowing those likely would be his last games for the Cubs. (He would go 3-for-11 in the three games, including a double, lifting his average to .193. His final hit: a single off Ken Reynolds in the third game, in front of 18,505 at Wrigley Field.)

In early November, the Cubs announced Banks would become a full-time first-base coach. There were some rumors that Banks could take over for Durocher as manager. Cubs owner Philip K. Wrigley squashed that.

"Managing is a dirty job, it doesn't last long, and it certainly isn't anything I would wish on Banks, who is headed for baseball's Hall of Fame," Wrigley told the *Chicago Tribune* on November 10, 1971. "I'm too fond of Ernie to make him manager of anything."

Banks was voted into the Hall in 1977, his first year of eligibility. He became an ambassador for the Cubs, throwing out the first pitch for the 1990 All-Star Game played at Wrigley Field. In 2013, Banks was awarded the Presidential Medal of Freedom by President Barack Obama.

Ernie Banks hit 512 home runs, won two MVP awards, was a 14-time All-Star, and would sing if asked. Teammate Billy Williams called Mr. Cub "a joy to be around."

"That's Mr. Cub—the man who came up through the Negro Leagues, making $7 a day, and became the first Black player to suit up for the Cubs and one of the greatest hitters of all time," Obama said during the ceremony at the White House. "In the process Ernie became known as much for his 512 home runs as for his cheer, his optimism, and his eternal faith that someday the Cubs would go all the way."

Teammate Billy Williams went with Banks to the White House. The two met in spring training in 1958 and became close friends.

"A lot of people can learn from what he did," Williams told me. "He'd come to spring training and come into the clubhouse and sit around and talk to the guys.... A lot of people saw him and knew he was a positive guy and that he knew the game of baseball."

The Cubs retired Banks' No. 14 in 1982—the first Cub to be so honored—and dedicated a statue of him outside Wrigley Field in March 2008.

In January 2015, a week shy of his 84th birthday, Ernie Banks passed away.

Williams said he was always asked if Banks' upbeat attitude was genuine.

"I'd say from the minute he woke up to the minute he went to bed," Williams said, "he's the same way with a positive attitude and a joy to be around."

Mr. Cub is buried three miles north of Wrigley, his grave next to Lake Willowmere in Graceland Cemetery.

Also buried at Graceland: architect Ludwig Mies van der Rohe and William Hulbert, part owner of the Chicago White Stockings, which later became the Cubs. Heavyweight champion boxer Jack Johnson is there, too, as well as retail giant Marshall Field.

Imagine the conversations they could be having. The songs they could be singing.

3

20-K GAME

Kerry Wood was having a tough time with his command while warming up at Wrigley Field before his fifth big-league start on May 6, 1998, so he sat down early in the bullpen.

"I was loose," Wood said. "I figured it was only going to get worse. It was an ugly warmup."

He'd opened the season at Triple-A Iowa because the Cubs had decided before spring training began that the right-handed pitcher would not be on their Opening Day roster. The team's first-round draft pick in 1995, Wood had overpowered batters in the minor leagues, but the Cubs felt they had five good starting pitchers and that the 20-year-old needed more experience.

In his last spring outing in Arizona, Wood faced the Angels. Anaheim manager Terry Collins saw enough. He predicted the Cubs would win the World Series that year.

"If you've got five pitchers better than Kerry Wood, you're going all the way," Collins said.

Wood showed he was ready on that May day when he pitched one of the most dominant games ever.

It was 71 degrees, cloudy, and dry at the start for the second game of a two-game series against the Houston Astros at Wrigley Field. Wood was paired with catcher Sandy Martinez for the first time. His first pitch of the game struck home-plate umpire Jerry Meals' mask.

"From my standpoint, I'd gone 50 pitches in the bullpen and didn't throw one strike," Wood said, "and the first pitch of the game, I hit the umpire in the mask, and I'm like, 'Here we go.'"

But he regrouped and struck out Craig Biggio, Derek Bell, and Jeff Bagwell in the first. Astros starter Shane Reynolds matched that in the Cubs' half. Wood then struck out Jack Howell and Moises Alou in the second and got Dave Clark to fly out.

Fans in the left field bleachers started holding up "K" signs for each one of Wood's strikeouts. A high school teacher had brought 16 cards to Wrigley. Little did he know that 16 wouldn't be enough.

Ricky Gutierrez singled to lead off the Astros' third, bouncing the ball past third baseman Kevin Orie. "Nobody said a thing," official scorer Don Friske told me. "Everybody just assumed it was a hit."

If you were one of the 15,758 at Wrigley that day and saw it, you most likely didn't question the call, either.

"Then," Wood said, "I got locked in with Sandy. There was nothing else going on around me other than his catcher's mitt and him. Guys talk about getting locked in and getting in the zone. It was a pretty cool feeling."

Wood struck out Brad Ausmus and escaped that inning, got Bagwell and Howell looking at strike three in the fourth, then struck out the side in the fifth. Reynolds fanned in the sixth, the 12th strikeout for Wood, which matched his personal best. He'd never struck out more than a dozen in a game at any level.

The rookie struck out the side again in the seventh and eighth innings to raise his total to 18, the most by any Cubs pitcher in franchise history. Two fans in the left field bleachers had agreed to have the letter "K" painted on their chests to keep the count accurate. The crowd was getting louder, especially when Wood had two strikes on a batter.

And at that point, there was some discussion in the press box. Wood would still have a no-hitter if not for that third-inning single.

"I had a couple people come up and say, 'Are you thinking of changing that?'" Friske said. "I said, 'No.'"

Wood wasn't keeping count of the strikeouts and neither was Martinez, but the catcher did see the K-signs in left field.

"In the seventh inning, for some reason I looked to left field and the bleachers and saw all the 'Ks' and said, 'Damn, we got so many,'" Martinez said. "The only thing I had in my mind was to try to win the game."

There was a light drizzle at Wrigley when Wood opened the ninth by striking out pinch-hitter Bill Spiers, then got Biggio to ground out to shortstop Jeff Blauser. Derek Bell whiffed for strikeout No. 20. Cubs win 2–0.

Wood pumped his fist after his last pitch, but not because he'd set a record for most strikeouts by a National League pitcher or a rookie pitcher and had matched the major league mark held by Roger Clemens. He wasn't aware of any of that.

Kerry Wood's first pitch of his 20-strikeout game in May 1998 was a little wild and hit the umpire. But he settled down and made history. (Getty Images)

Wood celebrated because he didn't walk a batter.

"I'd never had an outing when I didn't walk anybody, and everybody was talking about my walks for my entire minor league career," Wood said. "And I'd never had a complete game. I had a chance to go for a complete game and my thoughts were on no walks."

Did Wood have a favorite strikeout?

"Spiers was the one," Wood said of the ninth-inning leadoff at-bat. "The strikeout pitch was a slider and the worst one of the day, and I got around it, but it went straight sideways. By the time he finished swinging at it, from my point of view, Sandy's glove was behind him. The way it broke and the way it ended, I liked that one the best."

What about Gutierrez's hit?

"The only way Kevin gets that ball is if he lays out and dives," Wood said. "At that point, Ricky probably still had decent wheels, and you're not going to get him on a slow-hit ball where you have to leave your feet. It was a base hit, base hit all the way."

Martinez still has the catcher's mask and glove he used in that game. Wood has a game-used ball, his glove, and his cleats. His hat and jersey are in the Hall of Fame in Cooperstown, New York.

That one game changed Wood's life.

"As a 20-year-old, you think you're invincible and can go out and do it and keep doing it, but you're not ready for the hype," Wood said. "I wasn't.

"It definitely was a defining moment. For me, it showed me that I belonged here, it's not a fluke that I'm here, I deserve to be here, I can compete at this level."

Wood would hit double-digit strikeouts in eight more games his rookie season, including a 16-K game against the Reds on August 26. But he had to be shut down after one more start because of soreness in his right elbow. In April 1999, he underwent reconstructive surgery that kept him sidelined for that entire season. It was the first of many trips to the injured list. Wood bounced back in 2003 and led the major leagues with 266 strikeouts—and was stellar in the National League Division Series against the Braves—but injuries continued to hinder him.

In an effort to ease some of the strain on his arm, Wood switched to the bullpen full-time in 2008 and became the Cubs' closer. He left via free agency after that season, and pitched briefly for the Cleveland Indians and New York Yankees before returning to the Cubs in 2011.

By the next season it had become increasingly difficult to get his arm ready. On May 18, there were rumors before the Cubs' Interleague game against the White Sox that Wood was retiring. There was no formal announcement. During batting practice, Wood and his son, Justin, chased balls in the outfield and toured the ballpark, even climbing into the center field scoreboard.

Wood had talked to Cubs manager Dale Sveum about retirement. He wanted to leave on his terms and face one more batter.

"It's one of those things where you know," Sveum said. "It's a time in your life where you make that decision."

Wood took out the lineup card, then joined his teammates in the bullpen.

With one out and one on in the eighth inning, Wood entered the game. The White Sox's Dayan Viciedo didn't have a chance. Viciedo fouled off a 96-mph fastball, then fouled off the next pitch, a curve, and swung and missed at a 78-mph curve. It was Wood's 1,582nd strikeout of his career, and his final one.

Kerry Wood had thrown his last pitch. He was 34 years old.

Sveum had been ejected earlier in the game, so bench coach Jamie Quirk went to the mound to take Wood out. As the pitcher walked to the dugout, Justin surprised his dad by running out to give him a hug. Wood then tipped his cap to the fans and made one more curtain call. And it was over.

"I had fun, I had a blast," Wood said. "I wouldn't trade anything in."

4

8-8-88

On the night before the historic first night game at Wrigley Field, the Cubs had a workout to make sure they could see. But they couldn't.

"You stood in the outfield and you couldn't see the ball come off the bat at home plate, the way they had the lights adjusted," Cubs third-base coach Chuck Cottier told me. "We said right away, 'We can't play a night game like that. They can't see the ball in the outfield.'"

The technicians tweaked the lights and fixed the problem. But nobody could do anything about the weather.

First, a little background: other major league teams had begun installing lights after the Reds did so at Crosley Field in 1935 and saw a huge boost in their average crowds. Cubs owner Philip K. Wrigley was open to night baseball in 1941. The light standards and the steel, cable, and electrical equipment were ready, but those plans changed when the Japanese bombed Pearl Harbor. Wrigley donated the 165 tons of steel and copper to the U.S. war effort.

When the war ended and Cubs fans didn't demand night games, Wrigley opted to let sunshine prevail. Day baseball became part of the Cubs' tradition, along with the ivy-covered outfield walls, the bleachers, and the manually operated center field scoreboard. If you wanted night baseball, you could go to the South Side. Comiskey Park, where the White Sox played, had lights installed in 1939.

In March 1982, Cubs general manager Dallas Green—the former Philadelphia Phillies manager hired months earlier by new owner Tribune Co.—lobbied for lights and said that if they weren't put in, "we'll have to think about playing in another ballpark." However, the threat to play night baseball prompted protests from neighborhood groups, such as Citizens United for Baseball in the Sunshine (CUBS), an appropriate acronym.

Illinois Gov. James R. Thompson apparently was a fan of day baseball and signed legislation in August 1982 that effectively banned night games, saying it would "impose an undue hardship on nearly 60,000 residents who live within a four-block area of the stadium."

The mood changed in 1984 when the Cubs hosted their first postseason game since 1945 at Wrigley, facing the West Division champion San Diego Padres in the NL Championship Series. The format was switched to allow for weekend day games in Chicago (costing the Cubs a home game), and there was talk about possibly installing temporary lights for the World Series—but that became moot when the Cubs lost to San Diego in five games.

Chicago Mayor Harold Washington lent his support to the lights, and in November 1987 he proposed a compromise that would allow the Cubs to play 18 night games at home. Washington died before he could see the results. In February 1988, the Chicago city council passed an ordinance that would allow eight night games in 1988 and 18 after that.

The August 8 game against the Phillies was to be the first under the lights. That's what it said on T-shirts and souvenir ticket stubs: "8-8-88" would be The Night. Major League Baseball commissioner Peter Ueberroth and NL president Bart Giamatti were there, along with more than 500 credentialed media. Hall of Famers Ernie Banks and Billy Williams threw out ceremonial first pitches, and the Chicago Symphony Orchestra played. Harry Grossman, a 91-year-old Cubs fan, flipped a giant-sized switch and proclaimed, "Let there be light."

And it was good.

Rick Sutcliffe started for the Cubs.

"As long as I live, I never will forget that first pitch," Sutcliffe said. "I tried not to get too emotional. As I turned to the plate to deliver, all I saw [were] 40,000 flashes going off. It was more exciting than my first pitch in the majors."

The Phillies' leadoff batter, Phil Bradley, tried to spoil the festivities by hitting a home run over the left field bleachers and onto Waveland Avenue. (Comedian and actor Bill Murray, in the WGN-TV booth at the start of the game, could be heard on the broadcast yelling, "Turn 'em off! Turn the damn lights off!")

WGN-TV then flashed a severe thunderstorm warning. Morganna, the Kissing Bandit, ran onto the field to try to give Ryne Sandberg a smooch. Sandberg, evidently unshaken by Morganna and likely unaware of the weather alert, answered Bradley's blast in the Cubs' first with a two-run homer.

And there would be rain. The game was stopped in the fourth, an inning short of becoming official, and never resumed. Both homers were washed out. Critics of the lights claimed divine intervention.

"I don't know what I'll get credit for," Bradley told reporters after the rainout. "I'll still get credit for being the first hitter under the lights. It's like it happened, but it really didn't."

Wrigley Field organist Gary Pressy tried to entertain the fans during the delay with his weather repertoire, including the Carpenters' "Rainy Days and Mondays."

"[Cubs marketing director] John McDonough said, 'Just keep playing—play anything,'" Pressy said.

What did the players do? Greg Maddux, Les Lancaster, Al Nipper, and Jody Davis decided to belly-flop on the wet tarp.

"We were just kind of hanging out in the dugout kind of enjoying the thunderstorm and the rain and all that," Maddux said later. "You sit there long enough, I guess you start talking about some stupid things to do—and that came up and we ended up doing it.

"I don't know who instigated it—but I'm glad I did it," Maddux said. "It was fun. It was fun, and 20 years later people are still talking about it."

They were fined $500 each by general manager Jim Frey. Cottier, the coach, said Manager Don Zimmer wasn't aware of the players' shenanigans. "We tried to keep him up in the manager's office," Cottier said.

The game was finally called at 10:25 PM. The next night—8-9-88—the Cubs played the Mets in Wrigley Field's first official night game. The Cubs won 6–4.

"We had a grand old time with the lights," Dallas Green told me years later. "I was the first guy who dared say anything about it. And I was the first guy who dared say that's the reason the 1969 team lost. And that's the reason we lost in 1984, in my mind, because we lost the home field advantage because the television people wouldn't let us have that extra game.

"The Cubs had to come into present-day baseball."

Green left the team after the 1987 season. Where was he when the lights finally went on at Wrigley Field? He had a talk radio show in Philadelphia and a few regrets.

"I think Chicago and Wrigley Field lost a little bit with lights," Green told the *Chicago Tribune* on August 9, 1988. "I felt we could survive and make our money with day baseball."

What changed his mind?

"I saw the emotions of the fans and what day baseball meant to them," Green said. "It's special. I think TV and baseball missed the boat on this tradition, and it'll never be recouped."

5

SAMMY SOSA

The first home run Dave Davison caught in the bleachers was hit by Ivan DeJesus.

"I still have it," Davison told me. "I got the ball signed by him."

But the player who convinced Davison to hang out on the streets outside Wrigley Field during games was Sammy Sosa.

Davison switched from sitting in the bleachers to standing on Waveland Avenue behind the left field wall when he noticed more home runs were sailing over him than landing in the seats. These were the days at Wrigley Field before the giant video scoreboards were installed.

"I figured out it's a lot easier outside than standing in what was then seven rows of the bleachers," Davison said about his pursuit of free souvenirs. "At that time, almost every home run was over your head. Even though there's 400, 500 people in there, still the odds are against you catching a homer in the bleachers. I think I've caught three in the bleachers. I said, 'I've got to go outside.'"

By 1998, Davison was an established "ballhawk," often risking scrapes and bruises in pursuit of the little white sphere launched into the air by major league players.

It was a good move.

Prior to that year, the single-season record for most home runs was 61, set in 1961 by Roger Maris. Sosa had hit 36 in 1997, but it was Mark McGwire and Ken Griffey Jr. who were considered the sluggers to watch after clubbing 58 and 56 home runs, respectively. At the end of May 1998, McGwire had 27 home runs, Griffey had 19, Sosa 13.

Then Sosa got hot.

On June 1, the Cubs right fielder hit home runs off the Marlins' Ryan Dempster and Oscar Henriquez for his third multiple-homer game in his last four. Sosa then connected in five consecutive games off five different pitchers. He belted three homers on June 15, all off the Brewers' Cal Eldred—no, the wind wasn't blowing out at Wrigley Field—and launched two in each of two straight games against the Phillies, June 19–20, to raise his total to 29. He added four more dingers to finish the month with a major league record 20 home runs.

"I would like to have another month like that," said Sosa, who trailed McGwire by four.

Sosa's hot June changed everything for the ballhawks. Davison had caught Sosa's 12th homer that season on Waveland Avenue behind the left field bleachers on May 27, but it was the only one he would snare that year.

"It was the eighth inning and I'm the only one out here," Davison said of that game against the Phillies. "It was an empty street. It came right to me, I caught it on the fly.

"In June, he hit more and more homers. By July, people were leaving the game a little early to get his last at-bat. By August, people were coming out of bars and houses, and by September, people were coming down here, planning on spending their afternoon on this street."

While the number of souvenir seekers grew to the hundreds, Sosa continued his power surge. Whenever he hit a home run, Sosa would hop out of the batter's box, then break into a trot around the bases. As soon as Sosa returned to the dugout, he looked for the TV camera so he could tap his heart and blow kisses to his mother, who was watching in the Dominican Republic.

He hit nine more homers in July and another 13 in August. Maris' record was now in jeopardy. With one month to play, Sosa and McGwire were tied with 55 each.

"He's the man in the United States," Sosa said of McGwire. "I am the man in the Dominican Republic."

Now, it was the Popeye-armed redhead from Southern California versus the smiling outfielder who used to shine shoes in San Pedro de Macoris. On September 7–8, they squared off at Busch Stadium. McGwire tied Maris first, hitting his 61st in the first game of the series when he took the Cubs' Mike Morgan deep.

The next day, with the Maris family in attendance, the Cardinals' first baseman made history with No. 62, a 341-foot line drive to left off Steve Trachsel. Sosa trotted in from right field to embrace McGwire.

Sosa also cautioned his home run rival: "Don't forget about me. I'm coming."

He was right. Sosa tied McGwire again, hitting his 61st and 62nd against the Brewers on September 13 at Wrigley Field, connecting off Eric Plunk for the latter. As Sosa rounded the bases, the ballpark's speakers blared the theme from *2001: A Space Odyssey*.

Outside Wrigley, there was a scramble for No. 62 as the ball rolled down an alley off Waveland Avenue. Moe Mullins, one of the regular ballhawks, grabbed it first but was pounced on, and during a melee, the ball was wrenched from his hands. Eventually, it was returned to Sosa and then given to the Baseball Hall of Fame in Cooperstown, New York.

"I've had balls pried out of my hand, too," Davison said. "It just happens. You get there at the same time, you've got it, and the next guy slaps it out of your hand, and what are you going to do then?"

Sosa and McGwire wrapped up the season in record-setting style. They were tied at 65 going into their respective final series—the Cubs were at Houston and the Cardinals were home against the Expos. Sosa hit a monster 462-foot blast in the fourth inning on September 25 off the Astros' Jose Lima for No. 66, but McGwire tied him 45 minutes later when he hit one in the fifth inning off Shayne Bennett.

McGwire finished strong, adding two more in each of his final two games to set the single-season record at 70.

"We gave it a good show—a very, very good show," Sosa said. "I was so proud to be there. I was proud to be the guy who went there and competed against one of the greatest, and that was Mark McGwire."

All those homers helped propel the Cubs to a second-place finish in the Central Division and a wild-card berth, but the Cubs were swept in the National League Division Series by the Braves. Sosa managed two hits in 11 at-bats in the three games, none of them home runs.

He did edge McGwire in the voting by the Baseball Writers Association of America to be crowned the league's Most Valuable Player. Sosa finished with more hits (198), RBIs (158), and stolen bases (18) than McGwire.

Sosa's tenure with the Cubs wasn't all celebratory heart taps. After 13 seasons, 545 home runs (of his eventual total 609), and friction between the slugger, his teammates, and management, including an early exit from the last game of the 2004 season, Sosa was traded to the Orioles in February 2005. The Cubs, who acquired utility player Jerry Hairston Jr. and two minor leaguers in exchange, were so eager to part with Sosa they agreed to pick up $16.15 million of the $25 million he was owed.

"Those were the most beautiful 13 years of my life," Sosa said in Baltimore when the deal was announced. "The Chicago Cubs fans accept me. I support them, they support me. Chicago knows that I love them."

Sosa was aware of the Wrigley Field ballhawks, who raised a Dominican Republic flag at Kenmore and Waveland avenues in honor of the outfielder's homeland in 1998. Sosa could see the flag beyond the left field bleachers from the batter's box.

"He said he appreciated it," Davison said. "He used to drive down here [on Waveland], and if he hit a homer out, we'd walk up to the car with a pen and he'd sign the ball. I've got almost all of his homers signed. I've got 21 Sosa homers and probably 15 or 16 are signed."

Davison has collected more than 4,000 baseballs in his ballhawk career. He started a secondary business, cutting up some of the balls to make jewelry such as earrings or necklaces.

"What else are you going to do with 4,000 baseballs?" Davison said. "You can't take them with you."

6

RYNE SANDBERG

He was one of the steadiest, most reliable ballplayers of his generation. He won nine Gold Gloves for his defensive play at second base, won seven Silver Slugger awards, and was the National League Most Valuable Player in 1984. He was inducted into the Hall of Fame in 2005. And he was a prankster.

The game that changed Ryne Sandberg's baseball life? It was on June 23, 1984.

The Cubs had acquired Sandberg in January 1982, although he wasn't the headliner in the deal. First-year general manager Dallas Green—who had come over from Philadelphia and knew the organization—traded shortstop Ivan DeJesus to the Phillies for veteran Larry Bowa but wouldn't agree to the swap unless Sandberg, then a 22-year-old middle infielder, was included.

"I can't believe the Phillies gave up Sandberg," Bowa told the *Chicago Tribune* after the deal was announced. "He'll play for the Cubs right now. A good kid, big kid. Only thing is, he's real quiet. We're going to have to get him to talk more in Chicago."

Bobby Dernier, traded to the Cubs just before the '84 season, first met Sandberg when the two played rookie ball in the Phillies organization. Sandberg, Dernier recalled, didn't say much.

"We'd go on 10-hour bus trips in Montana and up into Canada," Dernier told me. "Back then, the Walkman was big, and if you had a Walkman, you must have gotten a bonus when you signed. I had one, and Ryno did, too.

"What we did was match up and bought one of those dual connectors so we could plug into the same machine with our headphones," Dernier said. "I can remember being on a bus with him for 10 hours and not saying a word and listening to one disc after another."

What Green envisioned was the perfect combo to ignite the Cubs' offense. It was Dernier's job, leading off, to get on base, then try to steal—or at least give the impression he was going to steal—to upset the pitcher. Harry Caray dubbed them "the Daily Double."

"Ryno, he really flourished with a distracted pitcher," Dernier said. "If he could sit on fastballs, he was going to hurt you. In the '80s, having that distraction at first base, having a guy who was a threat to steal and could steal bases, it made the pitcher in the '80s game pay split-attention."

The 1984 season was Sandberg's third in Chicago. The Cardinals were at Wrigley Field on that June day, opening a 7–1 lead after two innings and leading 9–3 after 5½.

It was 9–8 in the seventh when Cardinals manager Whitey Herzog called on closer Bruce Sutter—the ex-Cub who would lead the league that year with 45 saves—to preserve the lead.

The Saturday game just happened to be the nationally broadcast NBC-TV "Game of the Week," with announcers Tony Kubek and Bob Costas in the booth. They thanked their support crew in the top of the ninth.

But Sandberg changed the script by leading off the inning against Sutter with a game-tying home run.

Wrigley Field shook.

The Cardinals answered with two runs in the 10th off Lee Smith on Willie McGee's double, his fourth hit of the game, which completed the cycle. Costas named McGee as the player of the game in the bottom of the 10th.

But Dernier drew a walk with two outs in the Cubs' half of the inning to set up Sandberg, who tied the game again with a second homer off Sutter.

The ballpark shook again.

The Cubs would win in the 11th on a walk-off RBI single by pinch-hitter Dave Owen, the last position player available on manager Jim Frey's bench and now a terrific trivia answer. This forever would be known as The Sandberg Game.

Afterward, Herzog called him "Baby Ruth."

"Sandberg," Herzog said, "is the best player I have ever seen."

Before the first at-bat against Sutter, Bowa had told Sandberg what to look for.

Ryne Sandberg changed the script—and his career—during a Saturday Game of the Week in 1984 when he hit a pair of game-tying home runs off Bruce Sutter.

"What I basically did was that I looked down and in, but I also, for one of the only times in my career, I actually aimed for the bottom half of the baseball to try and square it up," Sandberg said. "That's what I did, that's what my approach was. I caught the bottom part of the ball and lifted it out. I was as surprised as anybody.

"And the second one was an identical feeling, identical swing and with the same results," he said. "So that was even more shocking to me."

Over the years, Sandberg and Sutter—also now in the Hall of Fame—have had chances to discuss the game. The conversations are short.

"The first time [Sutter] saw me, and he still does today when he sees me, is say, 'Don't even mention it,'" Sandberg said.

That 1984 season, Sandberg was the best in the National League, winning the Most Valuable Player award over Keith Hernandez, Tony Gwynn, and Mike Schmidt. Sutter finished sixth in the MVP balloting.

Sandberg might have been quiet, but he also was sneaky.

"Ryno, he'd light your shoes on fire," teammate Rick Sutcliffe told me. "He would soak your shoelaces in rubbing alcohol and then put them back in your shoes so when he lit them, they just exploded. He took it to another level."

Sandberg didn't limit his jokes to the clubhouse. When players arrived at their road hotels, they often stayed on the same floor. A teammate would hear someone knock on the hotel room door, then open it—and a large trash can that had been propped against it would crash onto the floor, spilling its contents. Yep, Sandberg.

And other things.

"I think he would lay back in the weeds," teammate Doug Dascenzo said.

He may have been a jokester, but Sandberg was respected as well.

"It was nice to be able to sit back and watch and observe how he went about his work," Dascenzo said. "There's a guy who is a superstar guy who takes young kids under his wing and shows us how to play the game of baseball without even talking about it."

The quiet man let his game do the talking. After 1984, he really didn't have to say much at all.

"[The 1984 season] had a huge effect on me personally," Sandberg told me. "Personal expectations, expectations from the baseball world, the fans, maybe along with my teammates on what I could do on a baseball field and what was expected. I think most of that was myself putting that onto myself. That's how I felt about it.

"MVP in '84 along with my second Gold Glove and a Silver [Slugger] for the first time, first All-Star Game—a lot happened that year, and there were a lot of new goals that were set for myself and along with playing for a winning team and getting to the playoffs for the first time and getting a taste of that.

"Those were my expectations for the rest of my career."

Sandberg played 12 more seasons with the Cubs and made it known that the 1997 season would be his last. The team honored him with pregame festivities on September 20.

"I truly lived my field of dreams right here at Wrigley Field," Sandberg said in speech to the crowd of 38,313.

"He's the greatest second baseman who ever lived," Cubs broadcaster Harry Caray said.

But Sandberg wasn't done with baseball. He could have settled into a life of golf and watching his grandkids grow up, but he chose to pursue a second career as a manager—the hard way.

"I look on this as a stepping stone so one day I can manage in the big leagues," Sandberg said when named manager of the Cubs' Class A Peoria Chiefs in December 2006. "This is the start of what I need to do to prepare myself."

It also meant no more charter flights. He'd be riding the bus in the minor leagues.

"A lot of people pay money to ride the bus, and I get to do it for free," Sandberg said. "I'm totally up for it."

Dascenzo, who also had become a minor league manager, said Sandberg called for advice.

"I said, 'Hey, man, it'd be great. But I'll tell you one thing—you've got to stick up for 25 guys,'" Dascenzo said. "He knew that. We never saw that side of him per se as a player. He went about his business and was quiet. Sure enough, he took that advice and ran with it."

During his playing career, Sandberg was ejected once from a game. In his first two seasons at Peoria, he was tossed 11 times.

"Showing some emotions and sticking up for the players and being vocal is a part of competing for me," Sandberg said. "It feels good, actually. It feels like I'm doing my job. It feels like I'm competing in the game."

He spent two seasons with the Chiefs, was promoted to Double-A Tennessee for the 2009 season, and moved up to Triple-A Iowa the next year. In 2010, he was named the Pacific Coast League manager of the year after guiding Iowa to an 82–62 record.

Would the next step be the majors? Cubs manager Lou Piniella hinted that Sandberg would be in the mix to replace him when he retired. Some Cubs fans were eager to see the Hall of Famer take over. Instead, when Piniella retired ahead of expectations in August 2010, general manager Jim Hendry named third-base coach Mike Quade to the job.

Sandberg decided to return to the Phillies to manage their Triple-A team, rejoining the organization that drafted him in 1978.

"I didn't think it was in the best interest for me, the Cubs, or ownership," Sandberg said of staying with Chicago. "I didn't think it was fair to me, the fans, or Mike Quade to have the perception that I was waiting for the ax to fall in Chicago."

He did eventually get to the big leagues. After the 2012 season, Sandberg was named the Phillies' third-base coach, and on August 16, 2013, he became the interim manager when Charlie Manuel was fired. The Phillies were scuffling, having lost 19 of their last 23 games.

"There have been signs of lackadaisical play," Sandberg said at the time. "And getting the players re-interested in these games—remind them that they are meaningful games—I think will be part of the order."

The Phillies removed the interim label on September 22, 2013, and Sandberg was given a three-year contract, becoming the first Hall of Famer to manage since Frank Robinson took over the Expos in 2002. But the Phillies didn't respond, and after they took a 26–48 record into late June in 2015, Sandberg resigned.

"I hate to lose," he said, "and that is the biggest thing that weighed on me."

To those who recalled his Hall of Fame speech in Cooperstown, New York, in July 2005, his decision to walk away was no shocker.

"The reason I am here, they tell me, is that I played the game a certain way," Sandberg said that day. "That I played the game the way it was supposed to be played. I don't know about that. But I do know this. I had too much respect for the game to play it any other way.

"I love to play baseball. I'm a baseball player. I've always been a baseball player. I'm still a baseball player. That's who I am."

And will always be.

7

HARRY CARAY

Since he was in second grade, Gary Pressy knew he wanted to be an organist for a major league team. Growing up at 82nd and Sacramento, he would be in his backyard and imitate Cubs first baseman Ernie Banks' batting stance as well as broadcaster Jack Brickhouse. He also pretended to be the home-plate umpire.

Unlike most kids, Pressy opened the pretend game by humming the national anthem.

"Baseball was in me and music has been in me," Pressy told me. "I couldn't hit the 2-0 fastball, so I had to do something. God blessed me with this."

And then—*Holy cow!*—the Cubs blessed him with Harry Caray.

Caray is credited with popularizing the sing-along stretch, although he first started in 1976 with the White Sox. He used to sing along to the music in the booth, but White Sox owner Bill Veeck saw fans sitting near the broadcaster chiming in. Veeck secretly placed a public address microphone in the booth, and then everyone could hear Caray sing "Take Me Out to the Ball Game" with organist Nancy Faust.

Veeck didn't do it because Caray had a great voice.

"Anybody in the ballpark hearing you sing 'Take Me Out to the Ballgame' knows that he can sing as well as you can," Veeck said. "Probably better than you can. So he or she sings along. Hell, if you had a good singing voice, you'd intimidate them, and nobody would join in."

When Caray switched to the North Side of Chicago in 1982, he continued the tradition—and, eventually, with Pressy at the organ.

John McDonough, who began his front-office career with the Chicago Sting soccer team, had been with the Cubs since 1983 and was named Cubs marketing director in 1987. He had heard Pressy play while the organist was with the Sting; Pressy subbed at the organ for three Cubs games in 1986, and when McDonough was promoted the next year, he hired Pressy full time for the baseball team, replacing Bruce Miles (no relation to the sportswriter of the same name). Miles had lasted less than three years.

"I was happy to be there one year, two months, three months," Pressy said. "Wayne [Messmer] was the P.A. guy at the time. After the first three games, Wayne said, 'You're a veteran. You'll be doing this for 30 years.'"

He made it to 33.

What helped Pressy's longevity is that he deferred to Caray on how to handle the seventh-inning stretch. The two first met in mid-May 1987 when Caray returned to the booth after suffering a mild stroke.

"The second day, Harry says, 'Gary, how are you? Are you new?'" Pressy said, relating his first meeting with the boisterous broadcast legend. "Right there, I felt so comfortable with him. He took [the stretch] very, very seriously. Perfect example—one day we had trouble with the sound system. He comes in and says, 'Gary, what happened?' I said it must be the sound system. He says, 'So fix it.'

"We'd be losing 8–1—we had some lousy teams," Pressy said. "The fans didn't care. They're staying until Harry sings. That's the influence that Harry put on that song in this ballpark."

There were other songs, of course.

"Harry loved music and he knew music. He loved B.J. Thomas. I was playing, '(Hey Won't You Play) Another Somebody Done Somebody Wrong Song,' and he mentioned it on the air. He said, 'That reminded me of alimony.'"

Pressy's first Cubs game as a fan was June 30, 1964, not long after he began humming the anthem in the backyard. Larry Jackson threw a one-hitter in a 1–0 Chicago victory over the Reds. Pete Rose got Cincinnati's only hit.

He got his music genes from his grandfather, who had played the violin for fun and learned music by ear. His parents taught him about baseball. Pressy's father was a White Sox fan, and his mother was a Cubs fan.

"When they got married, my father quickly converted," Pressy said.

The Cubs' 1998 season began on a sad note at Wrigley Field. Caray had passed away in February that year, and fans lost their louder-than-life connection to their favorite team. The voice so many associated with the Cubs was suddenly quiet.

Harry's widow, Dutchie, was to sing the seventh-inning stretch in a tribute to her late husband at the home opener April 3. How would

No matter how lopsided the score was at Wrigley Field, fans would stay until Harry Caray sang in the seventh-inning stretch. (Getty Images) the fans react? In the top of the seventh, the crowd of 39,102 started to chant "Harry, Harry" in anticipation.

"Everyone had goosebumps," Cubs third baseman Kevin Orie said.

You couldn't hear Dutchie's voice as the fans joined in a rousing rendition as a tribute. And then Wrigley Field was hushed and a few tears were shed as a bagpipe version of "Amazing Grace" was played.

The heartfelt response by the Cubs fans at that home opener showed the impact he had.

"That moment made people realize just how big Harry Caray was," first baseman Mark Grace said. "I think he was bigger than anyone in baseball."

After Caray's passing, the Cubs kept the stretch tradition alive by having guest conductors sing "Take Me Out to the Ball Game." Pressy tried to meet with the person beforehand for a quick practice run. His favorite? Legendary Dodgers broadcaster Vin Scully, who had a beautiful tenor voice.

When the Cubs added video scoreboards at Wrigley Field, they would sometimes show videos of Caray singing. Fans cheered and sang along as if Harry were still there having fun at the old ballpark, imperfect as ever.

"He was not Frank Sinatra," Pressy said, "but irregardless, he wanted it just right."

And Pressy knew, for himself, when it was just right to walk away. It would be after the 2019 season.

"Time marches on," Pressy said, sitting in the cramped corner of the press box that had been his workspace for three decades. "That's a long time."

8

1969

They led the National League East at the All-Star break by five games with a 61–37 record. Fans jammed the bleachers at Wrigley Field, excited by the Cubs' chances of reaching the postseason for the first time since 1945.

Ron Santo and Don Kessinger would be All-Star starters. Ernie Banks, Glenn Beckert, and Randy Hundley would join them as reserves. Billy Williams would drive in 95 runs. Career journeyman Jim Hickman would hit a then career-high 21 homers. Staff ace Ferguson Jenkins would win 21 games and lead the league in starts (42, completing 23 of them) and strikeouts (273).

And Dick Selma, from the bullpen in left field, would do his part to get the crowd involved.

"When it got kind of dead, he'd stand up waving a towel to get them going," Williams said. "That was an exciting season not only for the ballplayers but for the fans here in Chicago. People had a lot of fun. We were like rock stars."

But the fun didn't last in 1969.

There was the Don Young game.

On July 8 in New York, the Cubs led 3–1 going into the ninth with Jenkins still on the mound. Young, the rookie center fielder, misplayed two balls that inning, and the Mets rallied for a 4–3 victory. Young showered and dressed in seconds, and was gone before the media arrived postgame. Cubs manager Leo Durocher said his three-year-old could've caught the two balls. Santo also criticized his teammate.

"Somebody said the Cubs weren't taking us seriously," the Mets' Cleon Jones told reporters. "Maybe they'll take us seriously now."

The next day, Santo held a news conference in his hotel room on the 10th floor of the Waldorf Astoria to publicly apologize to Young.

Durocher wasn't as forgiving and benched Young for the July 9 game. Mets pitcher Tom Seaver threw a one-hitter against the Cubs. The only hit: a one-out single in the ninth by rookie Jim Qualls, who was starting in place of Young.

The Cubs still had a 4½-game lead in the division at the start of September—and then they didn't.

Willie Stargell didn't help. On September 7, Stargell launched a home run onto Sheffield Avenue with two outs in the ninth, connecting against Phil Regan, to tie the game. The Cubs would lose 7–5.

The next day in New York, the Cubs and Mets were tied at 2 in the sixth when Tommie Agee doubled. Wayne Garrett singled to right, and it appeared that Hickman's throw home had beaten Agee—but first-year umpire Dave Davidson called him safe. Hundley leaped in protest.

"He was out," Williams told me. "That's why Randy jumped up in the air and Leo came screaming out. Later on, Agee said he was out. He admitted that Randy touched him before he hit home plate. Everything was going the Mets' way that year. Jack Brickhouse used to say, 'I guess God lived in New York.'"

And if the Cubs needed any symbolism that their luck had turned, it came September 9 at Shea Stadium. Santo was standing in the on-deck circle in the fourth inning when a black cat appeared in front of the Cubs dugout, then disappeared into the ballpark. The Cubs lost the game—and would eventually drop 11 of the first 13 games that month.

That five-game lead at the start of the month had vanished. The Cubs trailed by 4½ games on September 15 and never recovered.

What happened?

"People said that the heat bothered us, day baseball," said Jenkins, who was one of three starting pitchers Durocher leaned on. (The others: Bill Hands and Ken Holtzman.) "To me, I don't think a lot of those factors were true. I just thought we ran out of the opportunity to score runs. We had eight, nine hits and one run. We'd hit into three or four double plays—we just stopped scoring runs."

Banks batted .186 in September, Kessinger .192, Hundley (who would start 145 games behind the plate) .163, Beckert .211.

Williams didn't think his teammates were worn out.

"A lot of guys, they weren't tired. They wanted to win," Williams said. "I remember Leo said, 'Anybody in here tired?' Leo asked Kessinger—'You tired?' What are you going to say? 'I'm good, I'm good.' We were in a pennant race. I don't think you get tired when you're in a pennant race. A lot of people blame that but we just didn't swing the bats.

"Everybody kind of slumped at the wrong time," Williams said. "I think we played 13 or 14 innings and couldn't score a run."

The Cubs didn't shine in '69 but finished second to the Mets.

"It's a bitter pill to swallow," Jenkins said, "because of the fact that we were right there on the precipice of winning and we just stopped scoring runs, we just stopped. We got hits but we didn't score runs, and the Mets caught us."

It was a team and a year Cubs fans who watched and lived through it will never forget.

The only thing Santo's daughter Linda knew about that season was that the subject was taboo in the house. She wasn't born in '69.

"I never really asked my dad about '69 a lot," Linda Santo Brown said. "I knew it was a rough season. He said, 'I don't want to talk about it.'"

Linda loves seeing young Cubs fans wearing her dad's No. 10 at Wrigley Field.

"He said they didn't go all the way," she said, "but he got the best friends of his life."

9

FERGIE JENKINS

Ferguson Jenkins relished being named the Cubs' Opening Day starter. That meant he would likely face the opponent's best pitcher. And one of the right-hander's best games to kick off a season was against his rival, and fellow ace, Bob Gibson.

The wind was blowing in at Wrigley Field on April 6, 1971, making it feel colder than the 40-degree game-time temperature when the Cubs played host to the Cardinals. Gibson was the reigning Cy Young Award winner; Jenkins had finished third in 1970.

"That was a rivalry," Jenkins said of facing Gibson. "Whenever we went to St. Louis, I got him. And similar, coming back to Chicago, I knew I was going to get Gibson.

"I mean, that was a fun part of it," Jenkins said. "You weren't going to go out there and get a fourth-rate pitcher. You'd get the top pitcher, and I had to stay on top of my game."

Gibson had beaten the Cubs the last four times he faced them in 1970, but Jenkins had won five of his seven decisions against the hard-throwing right-hander.

"I always tried to get myself up against him," Jenkins said of Gibson. "When you have Cy Young out there against you, you always try a little harder."

Jenkins put together superlative stats during his 19-year career, which included 10 seasons with the Cubs. How did he do it? It's simple. He threw strikes.

He got that message from his first manager in the Phillies organization, ex-catcher Andy Seminick: never give in to the hitter. Hall of Famer Robin Roberts, briefly with the Cubs as a pitcher-adviser in 1966, repeated it: throw strikes, make the hitter do the work. When Jenkins pitched at Wrigley, he didn't worry about which direction the wind was blowing. He had to deal with Roberto Clemente, Willie Stargell, and Tony Perez.

A native of Chatham, Ontario, Jenkins played hockey, basketball, and baseball growing up in Canada. He was drafted by the Phillies, who

traded him to the Cubs in April 1966. Jenkins was upset at being dealt but drove all night to get to Chicago—and on April 23, two days after the trade was completed, he pitched in relief and hit a home run in his first game for the Cubs.

He was the Opening Day starter the next season. He would start six as a Cub.

And after his playing days, he would remain a presence with the team, notably in spring training.

Ryan Dempster was the Cubs' Opening Day starter only twice, in 2011 and 2012, and he knows the impact Jenkins can have. Dempster, who had been struggling with the Marlins and the Reds as a starting pitcher before coming to the Cubs in 2004 and being moved to the bullpen, estimated he'd tried 20 different changeup grips but none worked—until Jenkins offered a tip on a back field in Mesa, Arizona, in spring training 2005.

"He showed me, and then I was throwing a bullpen and I threw one and it went *phoom-phoom*, and [pitching coach] Larry Rothschild said, 'What's that?'" Dempster said. "I said, 'I don't know—Fergie showed me this grip.' Larry said, 'Throw it again.' And I threw it again and it went *phoom-phoom*, and Larry said, 'All right, we're going to keep throwing that.'

"We just kept working on it and it ended up changing my career."

Jenkins would mentor pitchers about the quirkiness of Wrigley Field and how it helped that he was durable. (He threw 300 or more innings in five different seasons and 270-plus in four others. Greg Maddux, considered a workhorse for his time, never threw more than 268.) He said he kept his arm in shape by throwing batting practice between starts.

"Guys throw on the side now or they throw long [toss]," Jenkins said. "I threw to the extra men. It could be seven, eight, 10 minutes, just to loosen my arm up again. That was the format [pitching coach] Joe Becker wanted his pitching staff to do. Kenny Holtzman did it, Bill Hands. [Milt] Pappas tried it for a while, and he didn't like it. I think Rich Nye did it. There were quite a few of us who had that opportunity."

When the Cubs won the World Series in 2016, their pitching staff compiled the best ERA in the National League. The starters totaled five complete games during the 162-game season. Jenkins won at least 20 games six straight years, and in 1971 finished 30 of his 39 starts, including that awesome Opening Day game.

The Cubs opened a 1–0 lead in the fourth inning that day on Johnny Callison's RBI double, but the Cardinals tied it with two outs in the seventh on a solo homer by Joe Torre. Jenkins then retired 10 of the final 11 batters he faced, including Lou Brock, Torre, and Jose Cardenal in the 10th.

Then with one out in the Cubs 10th, Billy Williams—whom Jenkins liked to call his "old fishing buddy"—won it with a walk-off homer off Gibson, delighting the 39,079 at Wrigley. The hit was the Cubs' seventh off Gibson that day; Jenkins wound up with a three-hitter. Time of the extra-inning game: 1:58.

"I've never seen him throw better," Cubs shortstop Don Kessinger said of Jenkins afterward.

"I figure if you just throw strikes," Jenkins said, "you'll make them do half the work."

Jenkins would finish that season leading the National League in innings pitched (325) and complete games (30)—as well as hits and home runs allowed—and win the Cy Young Award Gibson had won the year before.

If you compare Jenkins and Gibson head-to-head, the Cubs' ace won more games, struck out more batters, and totaled more innings in his career. He just never pitched in the postseason; Gibson pitched in three World Series and was MVP in two of them.

"I think because he had so many World Series competitions and the notoriety, he was considered at one time probably the best pitcher in the National League," Jenkins said. "There was [Juan] Marichal, [Gaylord] Perry, [Tom] Seaver, myself, [Phil] Niekro—there were quite a few of us.

"Head-to-head, I had the upper hand," Jenkins said. "Billy Williams hit him like he owned him, and it was similar with Ernie [Banks] and [Ron] Santo. That gave me the opportunity to beat him. I beat him in St. Louis, beat him in Chicago. That was gratifying for me, getting the opportunity to pitch against one of the best.

"My ability was just as good as his. People come up to me and say he was the winningest pitcher—and I say, no, he's not; I'm the winningest Black pitcher in baseball."

Gibson would finish his great career with 251 wins. Jenkins would finish his with 284. Including the memorable one that cold April 1971 afternoon in Wrigley Field.

10

RON SANTO

Pat Hughes had spent 12 years as Bob Uecker's radio partner in Milwaukee, so he knew something about working with colorful characters.

Hughes and Ron Santo would debut as a broadcast team in spring training in 1996. The night before the game, Santo called Hughes.

"He said, 'Look, I know you're excited. You're going to be great,'" Hughes said. "We're going to have fun, this will be a great partnership and don't worry about a thing.' I hung up the phone and I thought that is very kind of him, very considerate.

"I slept well."

It didn't take long for Hughes to feel comfortable with Santo on the air. In their first half-inning together that spring, the Mariners loaded the bases with nobody out, and Cubs starter Frank Castillo escaped without giving up a run.

"Ron seemed to enjoy the half-inning, and as soon as Mark Grace caught the pop up to end the inning, I wrapped up the inning—'At the end of the half-inning, Mariners nothing, Cubs coming up. This is the Cubs radio network.' Ron then stands up and shakes my hand. You know how he was—he had that big smile on his face, like, *Oh, boy, this is going to be a great partnership.*"

It was. Santo and Hughes entertained Cubs fans from 1996 to 2010.

"I don't know that there's ever been a broadcaster who has been as big of a fan of his team as Ron Santo," Hughes said.

Santo was a popular player during his 14 seasons with the Cubs, impressing fans with his hustle, his heel-clicking enthusiasm, and his talent. He won five Gold Gloves and was a nine-time All-Star and a key player on a 1969 team that, despite a famously disappointing finish, remained especially beloved. When he became a radio analyst in 1990 (paired with Thom Brennaman), Santo didn't wear his emotions on his sleeve; he broadcast them on the airwaves.

Loyal listeners groaned with Santo when Cubs outfielder Brant Brown dropped a key fly ball in Milwaukee in 1998, and shared his elation when the team reached the postseason in 1998, 2003, '07, and '08.

"I always tell broadcasters, you kind of have to know your audience," Hughes said. "Our fans want to know about the Cubs and how it affects the Cubs and what's going on with the Cubs.

"In Chicago, it's more of a partisanship audience than perhaps anywhere else in the world."

Santo knew all about Cubs fans. He signed with the team as an amateur free agent out of Seattle in 1959 and made his debut in Pittsburgh on June 26, 1960, the first time he'd ever been in a big-league ballpark.

Two days later, he played his first game at Wrigley Field and fell in love with the place.

"It was so beautiful," Santo told me. "It was like playing in my backyard. It didn't feel like, 'Jeez, I'm overwhelmed.' It felt like, 'This is baseball.'"

Unfortunately for Santo, the Cubs didn't have that much success during his tenure. The highest the team finished was second, doing so in 1969, '70, and again in '72. But Santo wound up with a career .277 batting average and 342 home runs, and in an eight-season run—1963–1970—averaged 105 RBIs. He was successful despite battling diabetes, a disease he kept secret. Santo was diagnosed when he was 18 but didn't reveal it until the Cubs celebrated "Ron Santo Day" at Wrigley Field on August 28, 1971.

Santo would eventually lose both of his legs to diabetes, but that didn't deter him. It just meant he got a ride to the Wrigley Field press box in a golf cart. His prosthetics were designed to look like the Cubs' uniforms.

When he was done playing, Santo lent his support to the Juvenile Diabetes Research Foundation and sponsored a charity walk in Chicago.

Being around the Cubs certainly helped Santo cope with the debilitating effects of the disease.

"Did it keep him alive five more years, or 10 more years? I don't know," Hughes said. "I know he loved being at the ballpark, he loved being a part of the broadcast—and it was a very popular broadcast.

Pat Hughes, on his radio partner: "I don't know that there's ever been a broadcaster who has been as big of a fan of his team as Ron Santo." (Getty Images)

"It gave him something to do and it made him feel still vibrant and worthwhile."

Santo's daughter Linda knows how important the Cubs were to her father.

"Every spring, getting back into spring training and getting back into the season is what I feel kept him alive as long as he was," Linda told me. "It was always about getting back to the booth.

KEN HUBBS

On September 10, 1961, two rookies made their major league debuts with the Cubs. Lou Brock batted leadoff and started in center field, and his career took an abrupt turn in June 1964 when he was dealt to the Cardinals. This story is about second baseman Ken Hubbs, who batted second in the first of 324 games the California kid played before his life ended tragically at the age of 22.

"We'll never know how good he would have been," Ron Santo said of his young teammate.

Hubbs took over second base for the Cubs in 1962 and won Rookie of the Year and a Gold Glove, the first rookie to win the defensive honor. That year, he set a major league record for most consecutive errorless games (78) and most consecutive errorless chances (418) by a second baseman.

When he finally did commit an error in the eighth inning on September 5 in the second game of a doubleheader against the Reds, Hubbs could relax.

"I'm sure glad that's over with," Hubbs said after the game. "It was sort of like waiting for the other shoe to drop. Now I finally can concentrate on my hitting. Boy, I wasn't thinking at all at bat during the last few weeks. I was happy to break the record, and I'm glad it's all over with. Now I can go back to playing second base again."

The glove he used was donated to the Baseball Hall of Fame in Cooperstown.

"At the time he died, I definitely felt he was on his way to a Hall of Fame career," Cubs broadcaster Lou Boudreau said.

On February 13, 1964, Hubbs and a friend, Dennis Doyle, 23, took off from the Provo, Utah, airport in Hubbs' new Cessna 172. They were headed for Colton, California, Hubbs' hometown, but Hubbs turned the plane around shortly after takeoff. A storm overtook them and the plane dove into Utah Lake, just five miles from Provo.

"With every operation they had with his legs, all he would say to doctors is, 'What will get me back to the booth the fastest? If I have to learn how to walk on two prosthetics and I need to go to a healthcare facility and stay there for four weeks until I figure it out, if that's going to be the fastest way to get me to spring training, I'll do it.' It's what kept his spirit going."

Their bodies were found in the wreckage two days later.

"We were always joking—trying to convert each other," Santo said. "I'm Catholic, he was a Mormon. But after he died, I had to see a priest. I couldn't understand it. I mean, he loved life. He was a great human being. This was a kid who didn't even smoke or drink. Why him?"

Santo was one of the Cubs players who were pallbearers at the funeral, joining Ernie Banks, Glen Hobbie, Don Elston, Dick Ellsworth, and manager Bob Kennedy.

Hubbs was diagnosed with a ruptured hernia when he was only a few months old and had to wear a truss for five years. Doctors told his parents that their son would never be active. The doctors were wrong.

He played in the Little League World Series in 1954. He was recruited by Notre Dame to play quarterback. His family thought Hubbs would focus on basketball. The Cubs offered him $50,000 to sign and he did, then finished his education by attending classes at Brigham Young in the offseason.

On June 26, 2002, at Wrigley Field, the Cubs honored Hubbs' memory with a Ken Hubbs Memorial day. His older brother, Keith, had named his first son after Ken, and young Ken threw out the first pitch.

The city of Colton didn't forget its star athlete and named the high school gym after him. Each year, the Ken Hubbs Award is presented to the top male and female athlete in the area by a foundation established by the family.

The award winners are determined not only by their athletic achievement but also community involvement and service and their commitment to further their education.

After the Little League World Series in '54, the Hubbs family took a train back to California and stopped in Chicago long enough to see a Cubs game at Wrigley. Banks, in only his second big-league season, was the starting shortstop.

Little did they know that Banks would one day be a teammate—and a pallbearer.

On December 2, 2010, Ron Santo finally lost the battle. In August 2011, the Cubs unveiled a statue of the third baseman outside Wrigley Field. His No. 10 had been retired in 2003.

"Ron Santo was the backbone of the Chicago Cubs," teammate Ferguson Jenkins said during the statue ceremony. "When you think about pitching, you wanted No. 10 on that right side of the infield."

Santo may not have been around for the Cubs' 2016 World Series, but the team had a ring made for him and his family. Linda and her two sons were on their way to Chicago when they met a woman at the Phoenix airport who noticed they were wearing Cubs gear.

"She said, 'I used to like the Cubs,'" Linda said. "I said, 'Are you a Diamondbacks fan now?' She says, 'No, I don't watch any of them. The players these days are different.' She said, 'It's not like the way it used to be, like Ron Santo. I don't know if you know him.' And I'm like, 'That's my dad!'"

Santo showed his passion for the Cubs both as a player and broadcaster.

"I think Ron as a player gave the fans everything he had every day," Hughes said, "and I think as a broadcaster, he wanted them to win as badly as he possibly could each and every day."

Santo's wife, Vicki, saw it firsthand.

"After a loss, he'd come home, and I'd try to make him feel a little better and say, 'There's nothing you can do about the result of the game,'" she said. "'All you have to do is announce the game.'

"Well, he would turn and look at me and go, 'Vicki, I am a Cub.' That said it all."

11

GREG
MADDUX

Greg Maddux tried to throw hard. That may be difficult to believe for anyone who saw Maddux pitch, but when he was young and still learning his craft in the Cubs' minor league system, he'd try to blow hitters away.

It didn't work.

It wasn't until he played winter ball in Venezuela after the 1987 season that Maddux learned the importance of location over velocity. Cubs pitching coach Dick Pole was there and worked with the young right-hander.

What Maddux discovered was that the best pitch was a well-located fastball.

"If you want to find the definition of a pitcher, it's going to be Greg Maddux," Pole said. "It's not 'stuff' with him. It's location, pitch selection, changing speeds."

"It's too bad that all pitchers, that doesn't register with them," former Cubs third-base coach Chuck Cottier said.

Instead of trying to fire 99-plus-mph fastballs, Maddux switched to finesse. The result: 355 wins in a 23-year Hall of Fame career.

How good was his command? He is one of a handful of pitchers to finish with more than 3,000 strikeouts and fewer than 1,000 walks.

And he even has an unofficial statistic named after him: A "Maddux" is a complete game shutout in which the pitcher throws fewer than 100 pitches. Maddux did it 13 times in his career, including three games for the Cubs.

Cubs area scout Doug Mapson saw Greg pitch at Valley High School in Las Vegas—older brother Mike, another right-handed pitcher, had been signed by the Phillies in 1982—and wrote in his report that the younger Maddux would be a first-round draft pick if he only looked more like a potential major league player. (Even as a Cub rookie in 1987, Maddux was listed at 6'0" and a mere 150 pounds, easily the lightest player on the preseason roster; Jamie Moyer, another lean hopeful that year, was 20 pounds heavier.) Mapson did convince the Cubs to select

Maddux in 1984 in the second round—the 31st player taken overall—and it didn't take long for him to get to the big leagues.

Maddux actually made his debut as a pinch-runner in the 17th inning on September 3, 1986, against the Astros in a game that began the previous day but was suspended because Wrigley Field didn't have lights. Maddux then pitched the 18th but served up the game-winning home run to Billy Hatcher in an 8–7 Cubs loss. Said Cubs manager Gene Michael: "He made one mistake, but I like what I see in him."

When he first saw the slender pitcher in spring training, Michael thought Maddux was a bat boy.

Maddux's first big-league start on September 7, 1986, was a better indication of what he could do. He went the distance against the Reds in an 11–3 win and even contributed at the plate when he singled in the seventh.

"I'm kind of awe-struck now," Maddux told reporters after the game.

Jim Colborn, who was Maddux's pitching coach at Triple-A Iowa, projected the new Cubs starter as "a good competitor and he's fun to watch, especially knowing that he's just finished his paper route a couple of years ago."

What convinced Maddux that trying to throw hard wouldn't work?

"The hitters make it click with you," he said. "When you start throwing it and they start whacking it, that's what makes it click."

The lessons in Venezuela paid off. In 1988, Maddux won 18 games. The next season, he went 19–12 with a 2.95 ERA and finished third in the Cy Young voting. In 1992, he led the National League with 20 wins and won the Cy Young Award. It also gave him some bargaining power.

"One of the goals I set about four years ago was to win the Cy Young," Maddux said in November 1992. "To finally do that means a lot to me personally. It means all the hard work has paid off. Now the only thing left is to pitch in a World Series."

A free agent after that season, he wanted to play for a contending team. The Yankees, fourth in their division in 1992 but still the Yankees, were interested. So were the Braves, who were coming off back-to-back World Series appearances—both losses. Cubs general manager Larry Himes made his pitch to Maddux's agent, Scott Boras, who said they wanted to test the market. Himes knew he needed pitching, so he went ahead and signed Jose Guzman, Dan Plesac, and Randy Myers with the money that had been allocated for Maddux.

The Cubs' final offer to Maddux was a five-year deal at $27.5 million guaranteed with bonuses that would have pushed the total to $29 million. Maddux signed a five-year, $28 million contract with the NL champion Braves.

"This was Greg's No. 1 choice," Boras said when the Braves deal was announced in December 1992. "This is the reason he became a free agent—to carry with him the dream of being a world champion."

Maddux would win three more Cy Young Awards over his 11 seasons with the Braves and reach the postseason nine times, winning a World Series ring in 1995. The Cubs made it to the postseason twice in that span. No ring.

But Maddux did return to the Cubs when he signed a three-year deal in February 2004 to join a rotation that included Mark Prior, Kerry Wood, Matt Clement, and Carlos Zambrano. How excited were Cubs fans? The team sold more than half a million tickets in a single day when they went on sale later that month.

"I was a little bit crushed when they booted me out 11 years ago," Maddux said. "Now it's a whole new regime, and I feel honored to be invited back."

Maddux reached two milestones during his Cubs reunion tour. On August 7, 2004, he picked up his 300th win in an 8–4 victory over the Giants in San Francisco. On July 26, 2005, he fanned Omar Vizquel for his 3,000th career strikeout.

"It's monumental," Cubs pitcher Fergie Jenkins said of 300 wins. "I would say it's a ticket to the Hall of Fame."

What was most impressive was Maddux's consistency over his career.

"He's always kept his mechanics simple, and he's always kept his pitching style pretty simple—sinker, slider, occasional curve, and a changeup," said Joe Girardi, his former catcher. "To me, the most amazing thing about Greg Maddux is that he's the best student of pitching I've ever met. He paid more attention than other pitchers, and I think that's what has made him so great."

The Cubs knew how smart Maddux was, so when he retired after the 2008 season, general manager Jim Hendry hired him to mentor others in the organization.

At minor league ballparks, the majority of coaches watch the game from the stands. Maddux preferred the view from the dugout. It made sense. That was his vantage point during his 23-year major league career.

It was all about location.

12

BOYS OF ZIMMER: 1989 CUBS

No one knew what to expect of the Cubs in 1989.

They were counting on rookies Jerome Walton, Dwight Smith, and Joe Girardi and weren't sure how much more they would get from veterans Andre Dawson, Ryne Sandberg, and Rick Sutcliffe. First baseman Mark Grace was coming off a successful rookie season in which he batted .296, but—especially with another promising star, Rafael Palmeiro, traded—he was being counted on to produce runs. His rookie RBI total: 57.

Plus, they were relying on closer Mitch Williams (nicknamed "Wild Thing" for his stylistic—maddening?—resemblance to Ricky Vaughn in the film *Major League*), whom general manager Jim Frey acquired from the Rangers for Palmeiro and Jamie Moyer.

The '89 season was Don Zimmer's second as the Cubs' manager. Zimmer, a former Cub himself, and Frey grew up together in Cincinnati, playing at Western Hills High School. Frey picked his close friend to take over the team prior to the 1988 season, and after a promising start it had staggered to a fourth-place finish.

The '89 team didn't exactly generate optimism when it went 9–23 in spring training.

"We stunk," Cubs shortstop Shawon Dunston, who had been an All-Star in '88, said. "It wasn't like we were trying to lose. We stunk. But it doesn't count in spring training. It counts when the season starts."

Before the regular season began, Frey and Zimmer had dinner. After a few cocktails, Frey asked his friend if there was any chance the Cubs could finish .500.

"I said, 'Jimmy, if we play .500 this year, you and I will dance down Michigan Avenue together,'" Zimmer said.

It began...interestingly. In the season opener April 4 against the Phillies, Williams served up three straight singles to load the bases in the ninth inning, and then struck out the side, beginning with Mike Schmidt, for a 5–4 victory.

Williams gave Zimmer a few headaches. On June 8 at Wrigley Field, the Mets' Kevin McReynolds hit a game-tying home run off Williams in the ninth. But in that game, tied at 4 in the bottom of the 10th, the Cubs loaded the bases with one out and backup catcher Rick Wrona delivered a pinch-hit bunt single—a bases-loaded squeeze!—to drive in the game-winner and amaze the New York tabloids.

"I didn't want to squeeze on the first pitch," Zimmer said after the game. "I was afraid they might pitch out. Now [Wrona] goes up and fouls the first ball and I said I'm not going to take any chance. I'm going to go here and if they get me, they get me."

The Cubs players believed in Zim. He'd learned from his days with the Dodgers, where he began his career in 1954. Manager Walter Alston emphasized pitching, fundamentals, and doing the little things. Zimmer did the same.

Chuck Cottier, himself a former manager at Seattle, was Zimmer's third-base coach.

"He told me, 'Be aware for anything. I'm going to do things that I've always wanted to do. This might be my last go-around,'" Cottier said. "He said, 'Be alive for anything.' I think that year, we hit-and-run four times with the bases loaded. He was great at manufacturing runs."

Zimmer did like to take chances, but he also knew his players' talents.

"Zim would go off the game experiences that he had from all the years of being around it," outfielder Doug Dascenzo told me. "I remember running with one out on a 3–2 count. I was the runner at second and everybody was running. Grace fouled a pitch off and he went back and reloaded and did it again. Be ready for anything."

They got the pitching to back up the creative craziness on the bases. Greg Maddux won 19 games, Mike Bielecki went 18–7, and Sutcliffe finished 16–11. Williams—who, like his fictional counterpart, entered games at Wrigley Field to the Troggs' "Wild Thing"—saved 36 games.

"That was a season where things just fell into place for us," Dawson said. "We were winning ballgames we probably shouldn't have. Everything was sort of Cinderella for us."

Examples: pitcher Les Lancaster delivered a walk-off RBI double in the 11th for a victory over the Giants in July, and 10 days later, Grace—a left-handed batter with 13 home runs all season and not a classic power guy—homered off hard-throwing lefty Randy Myers with two out in the ninth for a 6–4 victory and sweep of the Mets.

"Unbelievable," Zimmer said.

"There's really nothing tricky to it," Grace said. "This team just believes in itself."

The Cubs finished with 33 come-from-behind wins in '89, including 20 after July 20. They clinched the NL East with a 3–2 victory over the Expos on September 26 for the franchise's second trip to the postseason since 1945.

After the win over the Expos, Zimmer called his coaches together in the visiting manager's office at Olympic Stadium. They were all soaked in beer from the celebration.

"That was a great day," Cottier said. "Zimmer had been in the game for so long, and after the game, he called us coaches in and gave us all a big hug and he had tears in his eyes and said, 'This is the greatest day I've ever had in baseball.'"

The magic didn't last. Grace batted .647 and drove in eight runs in what would be a five-game NL Championship Series, but Will Clark—who also drove in eight, including the game-winning runs off Williams in the deciding game—powered the Giants to advance to the World Series.

"I've had a lot of thrills in the game, but winning the division in 1989, clinching it in Montreal, was the biggest thrill I've had in the game," Zimmer said. "And that includes winning the World Series and hitting grand slam home runs.

"That was my biggest thrill."

13

2015 WILD-CARD GAME

The 2015 season was supposed to be another step in the rebuilding process for the Cubs. It was the first year of manager Joe Maddon's eccentricities—his slogans, wild animals, unorthodox lineups—and the players responded. Bolstered by their young talent and the top pitching staff in the National League, the Cubs won 97 games and secured a wild-card berth.

There would be signature pitching performances, but the biggest came October 7, when Jake Arrieta dominated during the "blackout" at PNC Park in Pittsburgh.

The Cubs had acquired Arrieta (3–9, 6.20 in 2012, his final full season in Baltimore) and Pedro Strop from the Orioles in July 2013, hoping a change of scenery would help the two pitchers. Arrieta was unique. He not only trained his body but also his mind and had started the visualization work while at TCU.

"Everybody here has the ability to throw a fastball down and away or throw a breaking ball in the dirt for a swing and a miss," Arrieta said. "But are we able to stay in that moment and understand what we're trying to accomplish and see it in our mind before we execute and then make the pitch? If you can see it before you execute, that only increases your chance for success."

He wasn't afraid to try new things to improve his performance. He squeezed a Pilates reformer device—a body-length workout aid—into a small multipurpose room at Wrigley Field the grounds crew used to monitor the weather. The Cubs also staged Maddon's news conferences there, and during one of the manager's pregame sessions, Arrieta ignored the reporters and did his Pilates workout.

On June 21 against the Twins, Arrieta threw a four-hit shutout and didn't walk a batter in the Cubs' 8–0 win. That was the day he became the ace.

"The seminal moment for him was the game in Minnesota," Maddon said. "He threw 120 pitches, and it looked like he took off from there."

Arrieta finished the 2015 season with 20 consecutive quality starts, going 16–1 with an 0.86 ERA in that stretch. The only loss came July 25, when the Phillies' Cole Hamels no-hit the Cubs at Wrigley Field.

Included in that span was Arrieta's first no-hitter, on August 30 at Dodger Stadium, which may be remembered more for his postgame outfit. That West Coast trip was one of the Cubs' theme trips, and the players and staff wore pajamas on the flight home. Arrieta had a close-fitting onesie adorned with mustaches.

"I don't take myself very seriously, other than when I'm out on the mound," Arrieta said. "I like to have fun and keep it light. [The onesie] got a pretty good rise out of some people. It was all in fun."

The right-hander posted an 0.75 ERA after the All-Star break, finished the season with a 1.77 ERA in 33 starts, and led the major leagues with 22 wins.

"He's unbelievable," teammate Anthony Rizzo said of Arrieta. "You get guys on base all the time, and they say they've never seen anything like it. It's a credit to him."

Added Cubs catcher Miguel Montero: "He's from another planet."

The Cubs had finished fifth in the previous five seasons—including a dismal 101-loss campaign in 2012—which made the 2015 season even sweeter. The Central Division boasted three teams in the playoffs that year, led by the 100-win Cardinals. The Pirates (98–64) and Cubs (97–65) would square off in a wild-card game at PNC Park. It was win or go home.

Jon Lester might have been the senior pitcher on the Cubs staff, but there was no question who would start in Pittsburgh. Arrieta was the best right-handed pitcher in baseball at that time.

The Pirates asked their fans to wear black that night to the ballpark to show their support. Arrieta responded via Twitter: "Whatever helps keep your hope alive, just know, it doesn't matter."

That riled up the crowd of 40,889 at PNC Park even more, and they tried to rattle the pitcher by chanting his name during the game. It didn't work.

The Cubs took a 1–0 lead in the first on Kyle Schwarber's RBI single. Schwarber, who was playing in the Instructional League a year earlier, added a monster 450-foot, two-run homer in the third off Gerrit Cole that cleared the right field seats.

That was more than enough for Arrieta, who struck out 11 and went the distance in the 4–0 win. When the Pirates' Francisco Cervelli lined out to second baseman Starlin Castro for the final out, Rizzo rushed to Arrieta and lifted him off the ground.

It was the first time a Cubs pitcher had thrown a shutout in the postseason since Claude Passeau blanked the Tigers on October 5, 1945, in Game 3 of the World Series.

Arrieta had faced the Pirates five times in the regular season, so they were familiar with him. He still shut them down.

"Jake is a different cat, man," Maddon said of Arrieta, who would win the NL Cy Young Award.

Winning the wild-card game raised expectations in Wrigleyville. The Cubs went on to beat their rivals, the Cardinals, in the NL Division Series but lost in the next round to the New York Mets. Still, getting to the postseason was a huge step in the young team's development.

"It was the most together, connected, selfless, team-first organization I've seen in a long time," Theo Epstein, president of baseball operations, said about the 2015 Cubs. "No one was trying to grab any credit or deflect any blame. They all supported one another.

"I think the whole was greater than the sum of the parts. That's magical and to be coveted and appreciated."

14

RICK SUTCLIFFE

It took a phone call from Harry Caray and a trip to Peoria to persuade Rick Sutcliffe to stay with the Cubs.

Sutcliffe first came to the team in a risky move by general manager Dallas Green in June 1984. The Cubs were battling in the National League East when Green decided to deal top prospect Joe Carter plus Mel Hall and two other players to the Indians for Sutcliffe, George Frazier, and Ron Hassey.

Sutcliffe was the Dodgers' first-round pick in 1974, but a spat with manager Tommy Lasorda—which included his flipping over Lasorda's desk—prompted Los Angeles to deal him to Cleveland.

Sutcliffe's time with the Indians did not begin well.

In spring training, he started against the Cubs in Mesa, Arizona, and the first batter of the game, Ty Waller, smacked a line drive to center. Sutcliffe tried to make a barehanded catch but instead ended up with torn ligaments in his right thumb—his pitching thumb. He didn't come out of the game right away; Sutcliffe had accepted a challenge from Indians manager Dave Garcia to report in shape, and the pitcher had lost more than 30 pounds. After all that hard work, Sutcliffe wasn't going to leave his first outing after one batter.

"I stayed in and threw one more pitch and I hit some guy in the neck named Sandberg," Sutcliffe said. This was 1982, and the guy with the neck was a rookie. "I had no idea who he was and he had no idea who I was, I'm sure. I had to come out because, obviously, I felt the pain in my thumb."

The Indians' medical staff told Sutcliffe his season was over before it had started and he was to go back to Cleveland for surgery. But athletic trainer Jimmy Warfield checked the X-rays before Sutcliffe left and thought the right-hander could still pitch.

"They'd put me in a cast, and I said, 'Cut it off,'" Sutcliffe said.

So the cast came off, and Sutcliffe went to the bullpen and discovered he could still pitch.

"There was some pain," Sutcliffe said, "but it beat the alternative of being done for the year."

He began the 1982 season in the bullpen, worked his way back into the Indians rotation, and finished with the best ERA (2.96) in the American League. In 1983, Sutcliffe won 17 games on a last-place team.

Spring training 1984 was progressing until Sutcliffe needed a root canal. However, the procedure didn't go well, and his tooth became infected. He lost 15 pounds in three days and felt weak, and his equilibrium was off. He kept trying to pitch.

"I finally had a decent game," Sutcliffe said, "and right after that was when I got the phone call from Dallas Green."

The Cubs had not been to the postseason since 1945. They had finished with a winning record only eight times since then, and 1983 wasn't one of them. Green, who had taken over as general manager after the '81 season, had already made a big move in late May of '84 when he acquired Dennis Eckersley from the Red Sox for fan favorite Bill Buckner.

"Dallas says, 'We want to sign you, but you have to sign an extension for us to do that. We can't give up these players knowing we might lose you,'" Sutcliffe said.

Sutcliffe was going to be a free agent after the 1984 season. He'd already decided where he wanted to pitch.

"I said, 'Dallas, when this season is over with, I'm signing with my hometown team, Kansas City,'" Sutcliffe said. "I said, 'I'm not the one who wants out of here. Bert Blyleven is the one who wants to be traded. Why don't you take him?' Quote-unquote, he said, 'I don't fucking want him,' and he hung up on me. I found out an hour later that he went ahead and made the deal."

The move paid off for everybody. In 1984, Sutcliffe went 16–1 in 20 starts for the Cubs, who won the NL East.

"It's unexplainable," Sutcliffe said of his success that first season with the Cubs. "Basically, the only thing that changed was the people who were around me. I had a better supporting cast."

In his first start for the Cubs, Sutcliffe picked up a win over the Pirates. He and his agent, Barry Axelrod, met with Green in his Wrigley Field office.

"Dallas was a man's man, he was bigger than life," Sutcliffe said. "He says, 'Hey, let's be honest. You didn't want to sign an extension then. You don't know if you like us and we don't fucking know if we like you.' He said, 'Let's wait until after 15 starts and we'll meet again and see where we're at.'"

After 15 starts, Sutcliffe was 14–1.

"[Green] called Barry and says, 'Don't waste your time getting on a plane. I know you guys aren't going to sign now. Rick says he's going back to Kansas City, but we're going to do everything we can to talk him out of it,'" Sutcliffe said of the conversation.

Sutcliffe was named the Cy Young Award winner in 1984. He was 28 years old and in demand by other major league teams.

"The season ends and [Yankees owner] George Steinbrenner calls and tells me, 'I don't finish second—you get the best deal you can and I'll give you more money and more years,'" Sutcliffe said. "[Braves owner] Ted Turner called and said, 'I need a pitcher and you need a team. I'll send you a blank contract whenever you want me to.'"

Sutcliffe and his wife, Robin, still wanted to go home to Kansas City, and the Royals also made an offer. But before Sutcliffe made a final decision, he had a commitment to honor. Caray, then the Cubs' broadcaster, had asked the pitcher to make an appearance in Peoria for his close friend, businessman Pete Vonachen. Caray called to make sure Sutcliffe was going and then delivered his sales pitch.

"Harry says, 'Let me tell you something. You can go to a lot of places for a lot more money and those fans will root for you and you will be in their mind,'" Sutcliffe said. "He said, 'You have ingrained yourself in the hearts of the Cub fans. They will never forget you, and you will always regret it if you don't sign back.'"

Vonachen, who owned the minor league team in Peoria, picked Sutcliffe up at the airport in an old station wagon that had a shovel and bucket in the back, which clanked as they bounced over railroad tracks. They finally arrived at a high school for the event.

"Pete was like, 'Oh my goodness,'" Sutcliffe said. "There were thousands of people there. It was Cubs fans. If you played for the Cubs, they were going to be there to see you."

Soon after, Sutcliffe called his agent and asked if he would meet him in Chicago the next day. He wanted to stay with the Cubs.

Axelrod's response? "I always hoped that would be your decision."

He stayed with the Cubs for seven more seasons. He never would pitch for the Kansas City Royals.

15

1984

The 1983 season was the 11th in a row in which the Cubs did not finish with a record above .500. It was time for some major changes.

General manager Dallas Green, who had taken over in October 1981, took a big step late in spring training in 1984 when he traded for outfielders Gary Matthews and Bob Dernier. Dernier gave the Cubs a legitimate leadoff man. Matthews was known as "Sarge" for a reason.

"We needed a screamer, a holler guy, a leader," Green told the *Chicago Tribune* about Matthews. "I mean, when I realized we could get him from the Phillies, I couldn't say 'yes' fast enough. This guy talked when it was time to talk and produced when it was time to produce."

Green wasn't done. The Cubs rotation at the start of the season featured Dick Ruthven, Chuck Rainey, and Steve Trout. The team was in first place on May 25 when Green sent fan favorite Bill Buckner, who won a batting title in 1980, to the Red Sox for starter Dennis Eckersley and infielder Mike Brumley.

"When we acquired Eckersley in May, that changed the locker room," Dernier told me. "When you lose somebody like Buckner, who is as influential as he was, and you get a guy who is as influential as Eckersley immediately, it becomes, 'Okay, we can get behind this because we got Eck.'"

But Green wanted more and in June made the bold move to deal top prospect Joe Carter plus outfielder Mel Hall to the Indians for starter Rick Sutcliffe, reliever George Frazier, and catcher Ron Hassey.

"I had a bias because [Sutcliffe] and I played against each other in high school," Dernier said. "I played with his little brother Terry in the summer. I said, 'Wow, we got Sut—he's a stud.' He was the No. 1 pick with the Dodgers and he was on a little bit of an exile in Cleveland. I told everybody, 'This guy is the real deal.' He was the best right-hander I ever played behind."

Sutcliffe had pitched five seasons with the Dodgers but he clashed with Tommy Lasorda, flipping the manager's desk in his office one day.

"That was Rick," Dernier said. "He was that kind of competitive natured guy. He had maybe taken on some false ego. He had that great rookie year and then he kind of fell off. He needed some proving ground. I think the Cub opportunity was that very thing, that opportunity."

Plus, this was the second time Sutcliffe had been traded. That can be a wake-up call.

"We all have that dream—I thought I'd be a Philly for life," Dernier said. "We all have that in the beginning and then reality sets in."

The Cubs still owned a 1½-game lead in the National League East when they acquired Sutcliffe, who made his first start six days later, posting a win over the Pirates. The big redhead would finish 16–1 in 20 starts with the Cubs.

And now with Sutcliffe, Eckersley, Dernier, and Matthews, plus Ryne Sandberg's MVP-caliber season, the Cubs would win the NL East by 6½ games with a 96–65 record. Not since 1972 had they finished a year above .500—and not since losing the World Series to the Tigers in 1945 had they been in a postseason.

"We were aware, no doubt," Dernier said. "We were more in tune with that '69 [Cubs] team and how close they came to doing the whole thing. We told them, 'Hey, we got you, we'll take that monkey off your back.'"

Though the Cubs had a better record than the West Division champion Padres—which should have given them the home-field advantage (three games at Wrigley if the series went five)—that advantage went to San Diego, because Wrigley Field didn't have lights. The television networks wanted the games broadcast at prime time in the evening.

"We'd earned it for the Chicago fans to get home-field advantage and see three out of five if that's what we needed," Dernier said. "I don't believe for a second we would've lost a game at Wrigley, not with that team.

"We bit the bullet and said, 'Okay, we'll go out and maul these guys anyway' and we kind of did—until we got to San Diego."

The Cubs romped 13–0 in Game 1 in the Wrigley Field sunshine. Dernier ignited the team by launching Eric Show's second pitch onto Waveland Avenue. One batter later, Matthews hit the first of his two home runs in the game, Sutcliffe—who started and went seven innings—added a homer off Show in the third, and the rout was on.

Dernier again provided the spark in Game 2. He singled to lead off, hustled all the way to third on Sandberg's ground-out, then scored on Matthews' bouncer en route to a 4–2 win.

"Don Zimmer had a great day," manager Jim Frey said of his third-base coach. "He knew Dernier could make it."

The 2–0 lead in the series should have been daunting for the Padres. The 1982 Milwaukee Brewers were the only NL team to rebound from a 2–0 deficit to win a five-game playoff series. Undaunted were San Diego fans; the Padres' airport bus had to be rerouted because more than 15,000 of them were partying in the parking lot to greet the team.

"And then," Dernier said, "we fell asleep for a game."

The Padres rewarded their fans—many of them wearing CUB-BUSTERS T-shirts—with a 7–1 win in Game 3 in front of 58,346, the largest crowd in team history. The Cubs still were just one victory from a berth in the World Series...but.

"I think the pressure is on them now," San Diego second baseman Alan Wiggins told the *Chicago Tribune*. "There's just too much history of Cub failure."

Frey didn't want to rush Sutcliffe on short rest—possibly projecting the right-hander would start Game 1 of the World Series—so he went with eight-game winner Scott Sanderson in Game 4. That didn't sit well with Sutcliffe or some of his teammates.

"A quality start for me has always been what Sandy Koufax told me, and that's when you shake the catcher's hand at the end of the game," Sutcliffe said to me later. "That's a quality start. [In Game 1] Frey says, 'Hey, you're done.' I said, 'No fucking way. I'm finishing this thing.' He said, 'No, we're going to bring you back if needed in Game 4.'

"Everybody including myself the day of Game 4 thought I was pitching that night. For some reason, Frey changed his mind. We all know the rest of the story."

Game 4 was tied at 5 in the eighth when Cubs closer Lee Smith took over and scrambled to hold the Padres scoreless despite a single and a Sandberg error. But with one out in the ninth, Tony Gwynn singled and Steve Garvey hit a spirit-crushing two-run homer for a 7–5 walk-off win.

And the series was even at 2.

In Game 5, the Cubs led 3–2 when Sutcliffe walked ex-Cub Carmelo Martinez on four pitches to open the seventh.

"It set the stage for their whole inning," Sutcliffe said.

Martinez advanced on Garry Templeton's sacrifice. A ground ball hit toward Cubs first baseman Leon Durham by pinch-hitter Tim Flannery should've been the second out. Durham dropped to one knee, but the ball skipped between his legs and into right field. Martinez scored the tying run. Wiggins singled, Gwynn lined a two-run double over Sandberg's shoulder, and Garvey followed with an RBI single.

The Padres won the game 6–3, and the series. They were in the World Series. The Cubs limped home.

"I give San Diego credit," Dernier said. "Those guys never quit."

And the monkey that rode the back of that '69 team? It stayed right where it was.

16

THE
HAWK

In the 1980s, the home clubhouse at Wrigley Field was narrow and small. Players had access to the showers via a hallway in the middle of the room, which also had a phone on the wall. When Shawon Dunston was first promoted to the Cubs' big-league team in 1985, his locker was next to the phone.

"I had to answer that phone and I hated it," Dunston said. "The next year, they put me between Andre and Ryno, the two quietest guys in the world. Combined, they didn't say more than 20 words a day, and I'm not exaggerating.

"I always like to talk, talk, talk, talk, talk, and they got me next to them—and that's when I learned how to be quiet and think about the game before the game," Dunston said. "That really helped me. I tell all the guys now, I was quiet when I played. When I went on the field, I was quiet. After the game is over, I'm loud. Before the game, I learned how to be a professional because of Andre Dawson and Ryne Sandberg."

Sandberg is celebrated in another chapter. Let's focus here on the Hawk, Andre Dawson.

An imposing figure at a lean, muscular 6'3", he played 11 seasons with the Expos and won six Gold Gloves, but the unforgiving artificial turf at Montreal's Olympic Stadium damaged his knees. He was desperate to get off the turf, and the outfield grass at Wrigley was natural and welcoming.

In spring training 1987, Dawson was still an unsigned free agent in early March and made Cubs general manager Dallas Green an unprecedented offer.

"It was a blank contract," Dawson told me. "It had nothing. Nothing. We just said fill in the terms. Whatever you think I'm worth, just jot it down on the contract and we'll respond to it. I just knew I didn't want to go back to Montreal."

Cubs pitcher Rick Sutcliffe offered $100,000 of his own money. Sutcliffe never did pay up. Dawson joked that the pitcher always said the check was in the mail.

Andre Dawson was a bargain when he first signed with the Cubs in 1987. The Hawk won MVP, and the respect of his teammates, that year. (Getty Images)

Green wrote down $500,000, and Dawson accepted.

It turned out to be quite a bargain. Dawson batted .287 and led the National League with 49 home runs and 137 RBIs in '87 to win the league's Most Valuable Player award. In six seasons in Chicago, he would make five All-Star teams. Fans adored him. Teammates and coaches were awed by him.

"The Hawk would have to come in and he'd be in that trainer's room for an hour before the game getting his knees worked on and rubbed on," Cubs coach Chuck Cottier told me. "As soon as he walked on that field, you would have never known he had two bad knees. Then after the game, he's back in the trainer's room for another hour. He'd limp

SHAWON-O-METER

There's one in the Smithsonian in Washington, D.C., and another in the Baseball Hall of Fame in Cooperstown, New York. Another is proudly hung on the wall of the Green Parrot bar in Key West, Florida, which is tended to by a devoted Cubs fan. And the most recent version was back in the hands of one of its original owners, Dave Cihla.

Whenever Shawon Dunston got a hit, Harry Caray would look for the Shawon-O-Meter in the Wrigley Field bleachers. Credit Cihla's friend, Jim Cybul, with creating the 30-by-40-foot sign that charted the shortstop's batting average, beginning on June 5, 1989.

Cihla had attended a Cubs series in Atlanta in late May and waved a bedsheet that said, "Go Cubs." WGN-TV's Arne Harris gave them some airtime on the broadcast, and their friends noticed. What could they do to get more TV time?

Dunston's batting average had just topped .200 for the first time that season after a game on June 4, and they'd read how Cubs pitcher Rick Sutcliffe gave the shortstop a baseball autographed by his teammates in honor of the feat.

Cybul, a graphic artist, concocted the Shawon-O-Meter and designed the sign, which made its debut in the bleachers on June 5 during the Cubs' series against the Mets. Broadcasters Caray and Steve Stone talked about it, the group got their airtime, and a phenomenon was born.

Unfortunately, the original sign only lasted that series. The weather, beer, and mustard all contributed to its demise. Cihla said they figured over to get dressed and get ready to leave and have to walk out of the clubhouse and up the stairs. He'd have trouble getting up the stairs.

"But as soon as he opened that door and walked outside where there were people around, he never limped one bit," Cottier said. "You would have never known his legs were bothering him. The Hawk, he was a great, great guy."

The other Cubs players saw Dawson's extensive regimen in the trainer's room and how he dealt with his troublesome knees.

"He played and never complained," Dunston said.

Dawson won Gold Gloves—on those knees—in each of his first two seasons in Chicago, and possessed a throwing arm that stopped base

their 15 minutes of fame was over. But Dunston's batting average kept rising, and after a big game, Caray bellowed on the air, "Where's the Shawon-O-Meter now?"

Cybul created another one, and he and Cihla made sure it was present at the rest of the Cubs' home games that season.

Dunston responded well, batting .311 in June and .356 in July. He finished the 1989 season at .278.

"What really turned Shawon around was when that fan started coming to the park with the 'Shawon-O-Meter,'" Sutcliffe told the *Chicago Tribune* in September 1989. "At first, we all got a chuckle out of it. Shawon was hitting about .200. It meant a lot to Shawon. He was very pleased that a fan would take the time to do something like that. That's when he started hitting."

The Smithsonian wanted one, saying it was "an excellent representation of the intersection of television and baseball fan enthusiasm." The Baseball Hall of Fame also asked for one, and it received the 1990 version. A third was given to the Chicago History Museum. Cihla, now a real estate agent, hand-delivered each one.

The Cubs had one on display at Wrigley Field, but in 2020 Cihla asked for it back because he was afraid it might be lost in all the historical memorabilia that the team has.

Cihla did meet Dunston at the 1990 Cubs Convention and has a photo of the two of them with the sign. There have been plenty of knockoffs, and Cybul and Cihla did create a Schwarb-O-Meter for outfielder Kyle Schwarber. But there's only one Shawon-O-Meter.

"It was," Cihla told me, "lightning in a bottle."

runners from even considering testing it. He also mentored the young Cubs—like Dunston.

In 1993, when Jim Lefebvre was the Cubs' manager, players were told they had to wear suits on the charter flights. When the team was in Montreal, Dawson took Dunston to a clothing store he knew and bought the shortstop five suits.

"Andre would buy us everything," said Dunston, who by then—with a $3 million-plus salary—could afford to buy his own. Among the veterans who had chipped in earlier: Lee Smith, who in 2019 joined Dawson in baseball's Hall of Fame.

"They took care of you and taught you to pass it down," Dunston said. "When I was a rookie, everyone took care of me because I was the only rookie on the team. I didn't have a roommate, so they took me out. There was an advantage to being the only baby on the team."

Dawson looked after Dunston like a father would for his son, which sometimes meant a little tough love.

"Before the game, he'd say, 'Shawon, you need to come out and run,'" Dunston said. "I said, 'I'm loose!' He said, 'Let's go out and run.' We'd talk about the game—what are you thinking about before the game, how do you prepare. I said, 'I'm going to try to kill the ball.' He said, 'You don't kill the ball, you meet the ball.' He said, 'Shawon, slow down. You want to meet the ball and have a plan.' I said, 'My plan is to get hits.' He said, 'Yeah, but what is he going to throw you?'"

Then they would discuss what that day's starting pitcher could throw and how Dunston should approach him.

Over time, it seemed as if Dawson was always giving Dunston lessons about the game—even when he wasn't around. Dawson's last season was 1996, but in 1999, when Dunston was on the Mets and playing the Braves in the National League Championship Series, those lessons paid off. The Braves had taken a 3–2 lead in the 15th inning of Game 5. Dunston was leading off the Mets' 15th.

"I kept fouling balls off and it was raining and pouring," Dunston said of his at-bat. "Andre Dawson just flashed in my head. I don't know why. It helped me relax, it helped me calm down. He's calm. I was like, 'Why is he in my head?' I had a 12-, 13-pitch at-bat and I got a base hit up the middle and the crowd went crazy at Shea Stadium.

"Then Mookie Wilson said, 'Shawon, you're going to steal a base,'" Dunston said. "I said, 'Steal?' He said yeah, and I did."

Dunston would eventually score the game-winning run.

"Everything was Andre that day, that time—at the plate was Andre Dawson. This is a true story.

"I tell him that, and he starts laughing. He said, 'Maybe you were listening to me.' Having me think about him calmed me down. I'll never forget that. He said, 'I'm proud of you.'"

Dunston, a coach on the Giants' staff after his playing days, would always have lunch with Dawson when both were in Miami, where Dawson finished his career and still lives.

"When I introduce him to the players, they all respect Andre like a god," Dunston said. "They say, 'Shawon, that was your teammate?' I said, 'That was my teammate for a long time, and he took care of me.'

"'You love him?' I said, 'Yeah. That's my big brother.'"

17

2003

The 2003 Cubs had plenty of star power. Sammy Sosa finally had a strong supporting cast, including Moises Alou, who drove in 91 runs that season. The Cubs' offense got a huge boost when, in a July 23 trade with the Pirates, general manager Jim Hendry acquired Aramis Ramirez (15 homers in 63 games as a Cub) and Kenny Lofton (.327 with Chicago) for fringe players.

Starting pitchers Mark Prior and Kerry Wood both topped 240 strikeouts, both totaled more than 200 innings, and both were All-Stars. Prior, the Cubs' super-hyped No. 1 draft pick in 2001, went 10–1 in the second half and finished with 18 wins; Wood's 266 strikeouts led the league, and though he only won 14 games, his 3.20 ERA would be his career-best as a starting pitcher.

Plus, the Cubs had a charismatic manager in Dusty Baker, who had guided the Giants into the World Series just a year earlier. The Cubs went 88–74 and won the Central Division thanks to a strong September surge, then beat the super-talented Braves in five games in the NL Division Series.

Next up, in the NL Championship Series, were the upstart Florida Marlins, who had won the 1997 World Series in just their fifth year of existence but began this one 16–22 under manager Jeff Torborg, who was then replaced by 72-year-old Jack McKeon. Wild-card winners, the Marlins went 18–8 in September—but nonetheless optimistic Cubs fans eagerly looked forward to baseball in late October, and hopes soared when the team took a 3–1 lead in the best-of-seven NLCS.

Even when the Cubs were shut down in Game 5 on a two-hitter by 23-year-old Josh Beckett, who struck out 11 in a 4–0 Marlins victory in Miami, the Cubs still were just a win away from advancing—and the series returned to Wrigley Field for Game 6.

Prior started and had a 3–0 lead going into the eighth. The Cubs were five outs away from their first trip to the World Series since 1945.

But with one out, Juan Pierre doubled. On a 3-2 count, Luis Castillo lifted a pop fly along the left field line. Left fielder Moises Alou ran to the high wall to try and make the catch, but the ball was deflected by a cluster of fans who did what normal fans do in those situations: they tried to catch a foul ball.

Alou slammed his glove, upset. Umpires ruled because the ball was in the seats—not in the field of play—there was no interference.

"The ball was in the stands," McKeon said. "The fan has a right to catch it." Then he added: "I don't think that was a turning point."

This was: Prior walked Castillo on the next pitch. Ivan Rodriguez followed with an RBI single, and it was 3–1. Miguel Cabrera hit a potential double-play grounder to sure-handed shortstop Alex Gonzalez (10 errors all season), but he bobbled it. ("Any time they ask about my career," he would tell ESPN nine years later, "it comes up.") The bases were loaded.

Derrek Lee delivered a two-run double. Game tied. Prior was pulled, Kyle Farnsworth and Mike Remlinger followed, and when the inning finally ended, eight runs had scored.

"We go for seven innings and Mark Prior is absolutely dominating the game," Marlins reliever Chad Fox said. "Next thing you know, you look up and we put a snowman on the board. I'm like, 'What the heck just happened?'"

"I don't know if it's a natural reaction to try to catch the ball," said Baker, who couldn't see the play from his dugout, "but if it's for your team, you have to give your player every opportunity and chance to catch it."

Alou saw it.

"I'm almost 100 percent sure that I had a clean shot to catch it," Alou said after the game. "But at the same time, I feel kind of bad for the guy because every fan in every ballpark, the first reaction they have is that they want a souvenir. But things like that happen. Too bad it happened to us, because we could be celebrating right now."

"I'm not going to blame the whole game on one play," Prior said. "We didn't lose a game because a fan jumped in [Alou's] way. Ninety-nine percent of the people, if you're in that situation, would have done the exact same thing. You can't blame him, and hopefully most people understand that."

Many people didn't. Cubs fans near the scene of the incident directed their rage toward a 26-year-old sitting in aisle 4, row 8, seat 113. Steve Bartman, wearing a Cubs cap and headphones, had been among the cluster—and had to be escorted from Wrigley Field by security.

As for Gonzalez, he'd been nearly automatic.

"I'm not going to fault 'Gonzo,'" Prior said. "Again, one play didn't cost us the game.... If I'd made the same pitches in the eighth inning I'd made all night, we might be out there celebrating."

But they weren't.

Bartman—harassed afterward by fans and by media eager for a scoop or a sound bite—went into seclusion, then issued a statement through a lawyer and excerpted here:

"There are few words to describe how awful I feel and what I have experienced within these last 24 hours," Bartman said. "I had my eyes glued on the approaching ball the entire time and was so caught up in the moment that I did not even see Moises Alou, much less that he may have had a play. To Moises Alou, the Chicago Cubs organization, Ron Santo, Ernie Banks, and Cubs fans everywhere, I am so truly sorry from the bottom of this Cubs fan's broken heart."

Forgotten by many, over time: this loss only tied the series. There would be a Game 7. Wood—who had won twice in the Division Series and, in this one, pitched into the seventh in Game 3, which the Cubs had won in 11 innings—would be back on the mound.

Wood hit a two-run homer to tie the game early, but failed to protect a 5–3 lead in the fifth, and the Marlins, with a 9–6 victory, would, again, be the ones celebrating.

In August 2009, ESPN issued a press release saying it was planning on producing a documentary that would attempt to answer the question: "Can Steve Bartman ever forgive Chicago?"

It was eventually titled *Catching Hell*.

It wasn't until 2016 that the Cubs finally did get to a World Series. And in July 2017, the Cubs presented Steve Bartman a world championship ring in a private ceremony.

Bartman, again through a representative, issued a statement, this time one of appreciation. It said, in part:

"My family and I will cherish it for generations. I am happy to be reunited with the Cubs family and positively moving forward with my life."

As of this writing, he still has not talked publicly about the incident.

18

LEE SMITH

When giant-sized Lee Smith lumbered from the bullpen to the pitcher's mound late in games at Wrigley Field, it was game over for the opposing team. The intimidating right-hander threw fastballs that were tough to hit and often tough to see because of the lengthening late-afternoon shadows at the ballpark.

"The shadows could've helped a little bit," Hall of Famer Billy Williams said, "but I don't think they helped him that much."

Williams is right: in 1983, when Smith was at his most unhittable as a Cub, his ERA at home was 1.99, on the road 1.29. Combined: 1.65. The spread was similar in '84.

What's undeniable: Smith didn't hurry when entering a game as the Cubs' closer.

"You didn't want to go rushing out there to face Mike Schmidt, so I was taking my time to figure this out before I got out there," Smith told me. "I think Mike Schmidt hit every day."

Smith figured it out most of the time in an 18-year career that began in 1980 with the Cubs. But it took some convincing to get him to accept the closer's job.

A native of Castor, Louisiana, Smith wanted to play basketball. A Cubs scout saw Smith in a high school baseball game by accident. The scout had been assigned to watch another player, who was a nephew of big-league pitcher Vida Blue. Smith had already committed to playing basketball at Northwestern State University, but the Cubs liked what they saw and selected Smith in the second round of the 1975 draft.

In the minor leagues, Smith was a starting pitcher. But in 1979 at Class AA Midland, his manager, former big-league catcher Randy Hundley, moved him to the bullpen. Smith resisted. He felt he was good enough to start and considered being a reliever an insult.

"In that day, the relievers didn't pitch until the starters got knocked out," Smith said. "I actually quit and went home."

It took an intervention by Williams, then a minor league coach for the Cubs, to get Smith on track. Williams traveled to Midland, and his message was direct: when Smith could get batters out at the Double-A level, he'd be promoted to Triple-A.

"Everybody saw great potential in Lee Smith," Williams said. "A lot of pitchers don't want to be relief pitchers. Starters had all the glory and were making all the money. It was a great turning point in his life."

"The toughest thing," Smith said, "was you felt you weren't good enough to start and it was so discouraging. You work all these years and now they tell me I'm not good enough to start and most of the great pitchers in the day were starting pitchers."

Williams convinced Smith to focus on baseball.

"I found out I had a better fastball than a jump shot," Smith told me.

The decision resulted in a Hall of Fame career. Smith would total a major league–leading 478 saves, a record that stood from 1993 to 2006, when Trevor Hoffman passed him. Smith was inducted into Cooperstown in 2019.

"I never dreamed of making it to the Hall of Fame," Smith said. "I was just trying to figure this pitching thing out and I was like, 'Man, I want to get to the big leagues for a couple years and maybe come back home and be a high school basketball coach.' That was my lifelong dream. I knew my family couldn't afford to send me to college. I was trying to get an education."

Smith had another reason for his slow, gangly walk from the bullpen at Wrigley Field to the pitcher's mound. Cubs day games started at 1:20 PM and if the game went past 4:30 PM, the grounds crew got overtime pay.

"He said, 'I'm trying to put your kids through school,'" Wrigley groundskeeper Rick Fuhs said.

Smith did prep a little differently than most pitchers. Growing up in Castor, he used to haul pulp wood, lifting huge logs onto the trucks.

"All the guys asked me, 'Hey, Smitty, what do you do to work out to get so big?'" Smith said. "I said, 'I hauled pulp wood.' They said, 'What they hell is pulp wood?' I said, 'You don't want to know and I don't want to talk about it.'"

He can still remember the smell.

When Smith finally did get to the big leagues and settled into the closer's role, he would take a little nap in the clubhouse when the game started. He knew he wasn't needed until late in the game. It was up to one of the assistant athletic trainers or longtime equipment manager Yosh Kawano to wake Smith up in time.

"For me, it couldn't have been a better city," Smith said of Chicago. "The fans there were so hungry to win a World Series. We came close in '84 and came up short. I think it was discouraging a little bit to not being able to bring it to Chicago during my days."

He joined the San Francisco Giants as a roving minor league pitching instructor. What did he tell young prospects?

"You just try to make things simple," Smith said. "I think now the kids have a lot more information than we did back in the day. We had a lot of on-the-job training. Now they have so much info, it's unbelievable the things these kids get information for. Learning the pitches, pitch selection, things like that. Back then, we just threw and tried to figure it out."

His career figures tell it all.

19

JOE MADDON

Flamingos. Cheetahs. Bear cubs, too. Magicians. Baseball-themed artwork and outrageous outfits on road trips. Bike rides on the lakefront. Onesies. American Legion Week.

Wrigley Field will never be the same after Joe Maddon's five seasons as manager. Fans should have known it would be a wild ride when Maddon revealed he interviewed for the job sitting on a Florida beach near his parked RV, "Cousin Eddie."

Maddon had just completed his ninth season as manager in Tampa Bay in 2014 when he discovered an opt-out clause in his contract, which kicked in when Rays executive vice president of baseball operations Andrew Friedman left to take over the Dodgers. Maddon made the move and became a free agent. The Cubs pounced. That season, Rick Renteria had led the Cubs to a fifth-place finish in his first season as manager and the third year of the team's rebuilding plan. The Cubs front office felt Maddon would accelerate the team's progress.

"We saw it as a unique opportunity and faced a clear dilemma: be loyal to Rick or be loyal to the organization," then Cubs president of baseball operations Theo Epstein said. "In this business of trying to win a world championship for the first time in 107 years, the organization has priority over any one individual. We decided to pursue Joe."

At his introductory news conference, which was held at a Wrigleyville bar because the ballpark was undergoing renovations, Maddon made quite an impression. The new Cubs manager offered to buy everyone a drink.

"Theo said I got one round," Maddon quipped. "That's a shot and a beer. That's the Hazleton Way."

Cubs fans soon learned about Hazleton, Pennsylvania, where Maddon grew up and where his mother, Beanie, still lived. Family was important to Maddon. He kept his late father's cap with him. The elder Joe Maddon, a plumber, had died in 2002, six months before his son, then a bench coach, and the Angels won the World Series.

As the new Cubs manager, Maddon said his first priority was to win the players' trust.

"It's much more important than cutoffs or relays, or this manual you may have to write, or scouting techniques or all this other minutiae that people want to focus on," Maddon said. "It's not rocket science how to play this game. It's much more difficult to trust each other."

The Cubs' new leader got his message across via numerous T-shirts, each sporting one of his "Maddonisms." Fans introduced the first one after that introductory news conference, sporting A Shot and a Beer, a silhouette of Maddon's hair and extra-large glasses. Maddon himself distributed T-shirts:

Never let the pressure exceed the pleasure.

Embrace the target.

Try not to suck.

Do simple better.

The process is fearless.

If you look hot, wear it.

But if players remembered only one, Maddon wanted it to be: Respect 90.

He asked players to run hard 90 feet to first base, knowing good things could happen. Andrew McCutchen inspired that saying when Maddon watched the outfielder hustle to first base during a spring training game in Port Charlotte, Florida.

"It doesn't take talent to run hard or play hard," Maddon said. "It just takes 'want to,' in a sense. It's going to start right there for us. We do that, and we'll be on our way."

Maddon knew when to give hugs and when to reprimand. He designated one week in August as "American Legion Week," when players would skip pregame work and just show up at the ballpark and play, harkening back to when they were kids. The goal was to create an environment that allowed everyone to relax and be themselves.

The environment helped advance the development of young players like Addison Russell, Kris Bryant, Kyle Hendricks, and Kyle Schwarber. Maddon wasn't afraid to make moves, and in early August benched Starlin Castro—an All-Star in 2014—and switched to Russell at shortstop. The emergence of Bryzzo—Bryant and Anthony Rizzo—plus solid pitching and motivational messages worked, and the Cubs secured a wild-card berth in 2015. They upended the rival Cardinals in the NL Division Series and reached the NL Championship Series, only to get swept by the Mets.

"Joe said 'playoffs' from the moment he was in a Cubs jersey," pitcher Jake Arrieta said. "As players, that's something you really appreciate from your manager to know he's all-in and he's not going to settle for anything less than the playoffs."

The next year, Cubs fans had high expectations that continued to soar after the team went 17–5 in April. The Cubs would finish with 103 wins, clinch the NL Central in mid-September, beat the Giants in the NLDS, and then take the pennant by ousting the Dodgers in the NLCS.

Led by a manager who meditated daily and thought outside the box, the Cubs now were in their first World Series since 1945. They faced the Cleveland Indians and were able to rally from a 3–1 deficit in the series to capture the championship by winning a tension-filled, rain-delayed Game 7. Some fans still cringe when they watch replays of the game and see Maddon pull starter Hendricks after 4⅔ innings, but the Cubs got it done, scoring the tie-breaking run in the 10th on Ben Zobrist's RBI double.

"We never quit," Maddon said after the celebration in Cleveland, and that phrase appropriately was engraved on the Cubs' championship rings.

They also had fun. The Cubs had plenty of unique guests over the course of the season, including some wild animals. Cubs pitcher Travis Wood remembered standing near Maddon before a game and asking about all the crazy creatures he'd heard about in the Tampa Bay clubhouse.

"I said, 'I need some of that. I want some penguins,'" Wood said. "And he got me a penguin."

Maddon will be remembered forever as the manager who brought a World Series to Chicago, ending a 108-year championship drought.

"Joe is a Hall-of-Fame manager," Epstein said. "He was the perfect guy for this team at the perfect time."

Epstein made that comment the day after Maddon's last game with the Cubs on September 29, 2019. Despite guiding the team to a 471–339 (.581) record and reaching the postseason four times in five years, Maddon's contract was not extended. In 2019, the Cubs finished third in the Central Division and missed the playoffs, and Maddon was again a free agent.

He was not out of work long, returning to the organization where he began his coaching career, the Angels, to take over as their manager in 2020.

Maddon and his wife, Jaye, took out a full-page ad in the *Chicago Tribune* to thank Cubs fans and suggest everyone "raise our glasses in a toast with a shot and a beer, like our grandparents and parents celebrated special occasions, or just a hard days work. Thank you for the past five years, for your passion, for your open hearts and minds, for forging everlasting relationships and for sharing your beautiful city."

20

RICK MONDAY

American flags are common sights at major league ballparks. There's one flying from the top of the center field scoreboard at Wrigley Field (as long as the wind off Lake Michigan isn't too strong). Huge American flags are often unfurled on the field during pregame ceremonies on Opening Day, the Fourth of July, and Memorial Day.

More than 40 years after rescuing one from being burned at Dodger Stadium, Rick Monday celebrates Flag Day nearly every day.

In 1965, Monday was selected first overall by the Kansas City Athletics in the major league draft and was assigned to Class A Lewiston. After the minor league season was over, he entered boot camp with the U.S. Marine Corps in San Diego and served for six months before returning to baseball in spring training. He fulfilled his six-year commitment as part of his ROTC obligation.

After six seasons with the A's, Monday was traded in November 1971 to the Cubs for pitcher Ken Holtzman.

He would bat .270 over five seasons with the Cubs, but what Monday will forever be remembered for was his patriotic save during an afternoon game on April 25, 1976.

As the Dodgers' fourth inning began, two people jumped over the left field fence and onto the field. Monday, who was in center field, was warming up with left fielder Jose Cardenal at the time.

"You don't know what's going to happen. Is it because they had too much to drink? Did they have a bet? All I know is something isn't right," Monday told MLB.com's Tracy Ringolsby in 2016. "Then I saw one of them had something cradled under his arm, which was the American flag."

The intruders stopped in left-center field and unfurled the flag like a blanket on the ground. One of them opened a can of lighter fluid and sprayed the flag.

"What I knew was what they were doing was wrong then, and it's wrong today," Monday said. "I had a lot of friends who lost their lives protecting the rights and freedoms that flag represented. I'm not sure what I was thinking except that I was angry, and I started to run after them."

The wind blew out the first match. Monday charged at them from center.

"My attitude was if they don't have it, they can't light it, so I scooped the flag up and kept running," Monday said. "I didn't know if it was on fire or not, but I did know one of the guys was not a [baseball prospect]. He threw the can of lighter fluid at me, but he didn't have a good enough arm to hit me."

The intruders—identified as William Thomas, 37, of Eldon, Missouri, and his 11-year-old son—were apprehended. The crowd of 25,167 cheered Monday's heroics and began to sing "God Bless America." He doesn't remember who won the game but does remember the singing.

"I still get goose bumps," Monday said. "The crowd reaction was rewarding. The fans made it clear they had a total dislike for what those guys were trying to do. The crowd reaction was inspiring."

When Monday came to bat in the top of the fifth, he received a standing ovation from the Los Angeles crowd, and the Dodger Stadium scoreboard flashed: "Rick Monday . . . You Made a Great Play."

The two men were messing with the wrong outfielder.

"If you're going to burn the flag, don't do it in front of me," Monday told the *Chicago Tribune* in 1976. "I've been to too many veterans' hospitals and seen too many broken bodies of guys trying to protect it."

President Gerald Ford sent Monday a letter of congratulations. Monday was invited to be the grand marshal of Chicago's Flag Day parade. The Illinois legislature proclaimed May 4, 1976, as "Rick Monday Day," and during a pregame ceremony the outfielder was presented with the flag that he had saved.

Monday gave a speech.

"I'd like to thank the State General Assembly for this very fine honor. I'd also like to thank Mr. Al Campanis of the Los Angeles Dodgers, and most importantly I'd like to thank the American public which to me typifies what the American flag represents.

"Those of us in Major League Baseball and those of us American citizens are not going to let people use our flag or the game of baseball to make any type of demonstration such as was tried. We've all seen,

FLAG DAY

Major League Baseball was shut down for six days after the terrorist attacks on New York and Washington, D.C., on September 11, 2001. The Cubs resumed play in Cincinnati on September 18 and played their first home game on September 27 against the Astros. Before the game, catcher Joe Girardi addressed the capacity Wrigley Field crowd as the team honored firefighters, police officers, and rescue workers.

"We have learned the true meaning of the word 'hero,'" Girardi said.

When Wayne Messmer sang the anthem, fans on the rooftops along Waveland and Sheffield avenues unfurled giant-size American flags on the front of their buildings. Sammy Sosa, who grew up in the Dominican Republic, amped up the patriotic feelings another notch when he held an American flag in his hand as he ran out to right field to start the game.

In the Cubs' first, Sosa jacked up the crowd again by hitting a home run—and he grabbed a small American flag from first-base coach Billy Williams and held it as he ran around the bases. The two had planned the celebration; it was up to Sosa to deliver the home run...

In 2020, baseball was again shut down, this time because of the COVID-19 pandemic. Racial issues had been in the headlines as well, with demonstrations following the death in May of George Floyd in Minneapolis while in police custody.

Clashes flared in several cities, including Chicago.

When MLB and players agreed to guidelines designed to protect teams from the virus, the Cubs resumed play at fanless Wrigley Field on July 24. That day, players wore T-shirts during batting practice that read, BLACK LIVES MATTER.

One of them was Cubs outfielder Jason Heyward.

"People want to throw out the label of a 'movement.' I'm not giving it a title," Heyward said. "I just call it, 'Let's do the right thing.' And I think that's what I can get behind always in my heart.

"When it comes to 'stick to sports,' I wish I could—but there's so many times that I don't have my uniform on that I'm treated like a Black man and not a baseball player. I have family. I'm going to have children one day, God willing. I am a child. I'm an older brother. I have grandparents. I've got cousins—Marines, military, law enforcement.

"I'm standing up for them. I can speak up a little more, and my voice will reach more people than theirs might."

And as he ran out to right field to start the game, Jason Heyward, who grew up in Georgia, carried a large Chicago flag in his hand.

we've all heard about the American citizens of the past who have not only given their lives but have given the service to protect the rights and freedoms each and every one of us has.

"If they don't want to do anything constructive to help this country become even a better country to live in and participate in, then also one of the rights that is available to them is that our borders are not guarded and they are free to leave.

"God bless America."

Monday said a phone call from a 15-year-old boy helped him realize the importance of his action. According to *Chicago Tribune* columnist David Condon, the boy told Monday he was at the game at Dodger Stadium with his parents, who were having a difficult time dealing with the death of his brother, who was killed in action in Vietnam.

"What made it really tough for the folks was that they'd never been able to understand what it was that my brother died for," the boy told Monday. "What was the sense? But when they saw you go after those men trying to burn the flag, tears came to their eyes. They wept openly.

"For the first time they realized what their son had been doing...why my brother had given up his life."

Monday and his wife have taken the flag across the country and used it to raise money for military charities. He is saluted on the anniversary of his heroics.

"Maybe I was thinking about the drill instructors from boot camp," Monday said of his motivation. "I didn't want any of them saying, 'Marine, why did you stand by and watch those guys burn that American flag?'"

21

ERNIE BROGLIO

Lou Brock was still trying to figure out the game when he was a young outfielder with the Cubs.

"I was a player with two left feet learning my way around in baseball when I was with the Cubs," Brock told me. It didn't help that the Cubs had a carousel of coaches, each with his own teaching plan.

At times, Brock flashed his speed and power and seemed capable of catching anything in the outfield. And there were days, like June 13, 1964, against the Pirates, when Brock couldn't get to a pop fly hit by Bill Mazeroski in time and it fell out of his reach in short center for a two-run double. The next day, Brock hit a two-run homer but also collided at first base with Pirates pitcher Steve Blass on a play.

"There were days I was outstanding," Brock said. "There were days that I looked like I never saw a baseball."

In 1963, Brock batted .316 against the Cardinals, and their manager, Johnny Keane, remembered—as well as a July 28 game when the outfielder drove in five runs and hit two homers, including one off right-handed starter Ernie Broglio, who was having an excellent season.

In June 1964, St. Louis needed a left fielder following Stan Musial's retirement. The Cubs and general manager John Holland were desperate for pitching. And on June 15—a day after Brock's adventures against the Pirates—Holland and St. Louis general manager Bing Devine addressed their respective needs with a trade that will live in infamy:

Brock for Broglio.

The Cubs appeared to have robbed the Cardinals. Brock was batting .251 and striking out at a prodigious rate when dealt with Jack Spring and Paul Toth for Broglio, Doug Clemens, and Bobby Shantz. The other names don't matter; Broglio was the star of the deal after winning 21 games in 1960 and 18 in '63. His arrival was heralded by the Cubs.

"I've been with this club four years now, and I've never had the feeling before that we could go all the way," Cubs third baseman Ron Santo told the *Chicago Tribune* when the trade was made. "With our pitching staff now, we can win the pennant."

The trade puzzled others.

"I've always thought Lou Brock will be a great ball player," Phillies manager Gene Mauch told the *Chicago Tribune* the day after the trade.

Mauch was right.

Keane gave Brock the green light to run (something he didn't have with the Cubs; he would steal 33 bases that partial season with the Cards versus 5 with the Cubs), and he batted .348 in 103 games to help the Cardinals win the World Series championship that year. He hit .300 in his first Series, including a homer off lefty Al Downing. (In 1963, his last full season in Chicago, Brock—a left-handed batter—batted .179 with no homers off southpaws.)

St. Louis would win it all again in '67 and reached the World Series in '68 only to lose in seven games to the Tigers. Brock's career World Series average: .391 with 14 stolen bases. He finished in the top 10 in MVP voting five times (including '64) and was elected to the Hall of Fame in 1985. Total hits: 3,023. Total steals: 938, including 118 in 1974, both then records since broken by Rickey Henderson.

Broglio? He was dealing with tendinitis in his shoulder at the time of the trade and struggled to make 16 starts in '64. In November that year, he underwent surgery on his right elbow to remove bone chips and a damaged ulnar nerve. He had three months of rest and reported to spring training.

"Last season was a big embarrassment to Broglio," head coach Bob Kennedy told the *Chicago Tribune* in February 1965. "Ernie's dead serious. He wants to prove that he belongs among the big winners. His spirit is high, and we're just hoping all these favorable signs will result in a big year for him."

But they didn't. Broglio won three games total the next two seasons, posted bloated ERAs, and pitched in his last game on July 2, 1966, in relief. Final hit off him: a two-run homer by the Phillies' Dick Allen.

"The worst trade ever? I have a hard time with that, although it sounds nice and makes you chuckle," Brock said. "Somehow people believe that."

Broglio didn't.

"The trade's brought up all the time," Broglio told me. "The bad thing about it, I went from a case of Budweiser to a pack of Wrigley spearmint gum. That's what really upset me. And a World Series ring."

Broglio told author Rob Rains that the Cardinals players called him during their 1964 World Series celebration party at Musial's restaurant. The pitcher had his own bottle of champagne and drank it with them.

As the years went on, Broglio handled his place in baseball history with grace and humor. He and Brock were invited to the 1995 Cubs convention, an annual fan fest held in the offseason.

"Do you know why I'm here?" Broglio said to Brock. "I'm here because of you."

"History put us together," Brock said. "We're joined at the hip."

Broglio died in July 2019 at the age of 83. Every story about him mentioned Lou Brock.

"Sometimes a trade is good," Broglio told me. "It turned out to be the greatest thing to happen to Lou. It backfired with the Cubs. If I hadn't been hurt, I think it would've been a different story."

22

BILLY WILLIAMS

Any conversation with Billy Williams will eventually turn to hitting. It's appropriate that it does. Williams was one of the most respected hitters in the game, batting .290 with 426 home runs in his 16-year career. He won the 1961 National League Rookie of the Year award and was the 1972 batting champion. Plus, he was durable and held the NL record for consecutive games played (1,117, since surpassed in the league only by Steve Garvey's 1,207).

"You have to hold a clubhouse meeting every time you play him," Casey Stengel once said of him.

The soft-spoken Williams grew up in Whistler, Alabama, and signed with the Cubs before the 1956 season. He had to learn about baseball and also life outside of Whistler. He couldn't eat at certain lunch counters because the space was reserved for white people only. He had to stay with a family rather than at the team hotel on road trips. The racial discrimination he experienced at Double-A San Antonio in 1959 was so upsetting that Williams left the team and returned home. Buck O'Neil, then a Cubs scout, talked the 21-year-old into returning, and the outfielder was eventually promoted to Triple-A Fort Worth, where he batted .476 (10-for-21, six of the hits for extra bases) before being called up to the big leagues.

Williams learned about hitting from Hall of Famer Rogers Hornsby, who finished his 23-year career with a lifetime .358 batting average, seven batting titles, and a memorable season in 1922 when he captured baseball's Triple Crown. Hornsby was irascible, but he connected with Williams.

"He talked about the strike zone and hitting strikes," Williams, later a Cubs hitting coach, told me about the early lessons from the infielder known as Rajah. "He really emphasized the strike zone. He didn't change your mechanics too much. The only thing he talked about was you have to hit soft out front like you're stepping on an egg. That allows you to keep your weight back. You always had the hands in a certain spot.

"Sweet Swingin'" Billy Williams learned from some of the best hitters and passed that knowledge on to today's ballplayers. (Getty Images)

"He would be in the batting cage until I got through hitting and he'd stay right there," Williams said. "At the end of fundamentals, we had an arm machine called the old 'Iron Mike,' and I would have to hit 10 balls in a row hard. If I missed one, I had to start all over again. At that time, you had to keep your eye on the ball. That's another thing he would emphasize, too.

"He used to sit right behind home plate in Chicago at Wrigley Field. If I swung at a ball, maybe I'd turn around and look at him and he'd always point to his eye—'Keep your eye on the ball.' The mechanics part of it, he didn't change that much. I had started to learn about hitting, and he wanted to keep that going."

Williams would give the same message to the next generation of Cubs players. Even after his official coaching days, he was a regular in spring training and hung around the batting cages to share his experience.

"His biggest thing was always being on time for the fastball because you can just react off everything else," Cubs outfielder Kyle Schwarber said of his chats with Williams. "You always trust your hands to react to everything else. You want to trust your hands to react to the offspeed and not take the fastball down the middle.

"Those are the things we kind of have conversations about, whenever he's down in the cage sitting there," Schwarber said. "Whenever you can talk to a legend like that about hitting, it obviously means something."

It meant something to Schwarber.

"He's been around the game for a long time, and with what he did in the game and how he dominated and then him transitioning to being a coach for a little bit and then coming around the organization a lot, I'm definitely all ears when he comes and wants to talk hitting."

The man known as "Sweet Swingin'" had his share of highlights. A day after turning 23 on June 16, 1961, Williams hit a grand slam against the Giants. He hit a two-run opposite field homer off Sandy Koufax on September 14, 1965, at Wrigley Field five days after the Dodgers lefty threw a perfect game against the Cubs. Williams hit for the cycle on July 17, 1966, against the Cardinals at Busch Stadium. He posted back-to-back 200-hit seasons in 1964 and '65. He contended for baseball's Triple

HANK SAUER

Long before Cubs fans cheered Sammy Sosa's home runs and just as Ernie Banks was about to emerge as Mr. Cub, they celebrated Hank Sauer's prodigious blasts and dubbed the big outfielder the Mayor of Wrigley Field.

Sauer played for the Cubs from mid-1949 to 1955 and won the National League's Most Valuable Player award in 1952, when he slugged 37 home runs and drove in 121 runs. He got news of the honor on November 20, the same day his son, Henry John Sauer Jr., was born.

"Everything good happens at once," Sauer told reporters that day. "Truthfully, I never thought I'd get it—the honor, I mean. We expected a son, of course. I'll have to buy a baseball bat for Christmas."

The adult Sauer wielded a huge, 40-ounce bat that produced enough power to excite Cubs fans even during those otherwise lean years. The left field bleacher fans who saluted his home runs by tossing packets of Sauer's favorite chewing tobacco onto the field needed an extra supply on June 11, 1952, when he hit three solo homers off the Phillies' Curt Simmons in a 3–2 Cubs win.

But Sauer's biggest blast that year came in the All-Star Game at Philadelphia's Shibe Park. The National League trailed 2–1 in the bottom of the fourth. Stan Musial was on first when Sauer—who started the game in left—connected for a home run off Bob Lemon. The NL won 3–2 in a game shortened by rain. Sauer also started for the National League in 1950, in right field, and drove in an early run on a fly ball.

(Sauer gave Simmons fits. The slugger's only other three-homer game was August 28, 1950, also against the left-hander in Chicago, one of those with a man on.)

The Cubs' best season with Sauer in the lineup was '52, his MVP year, when they finished fifth in the eight-team league. Still, he endeared himself to the fans—and his rationale applies today.

"You give the people of Chicago 100 percent of your ability, and they will love you," Sauer told me. "You strike out two or three times, hit into a double play two or three times, but if you run out balls, you run hard to first, the little things, they notice.

"That's how great the people of Chicago were. They were the kind of people who just knew. If you give them 100 percent, you'll never got booed."

Hank Sauer never got booed.

Crown in 1970, batting .322 (fourth in the National League) with 42 home runs (second) and 129 RBIs (second).

On June 29, 1969, between games of a doubleheader against the Cardinals, the Cubs celebrated "Billy Williams Day." In the first game, Williams tied Stan Musial's record of 895 consecutive games played in the NL, and then passed the Cardinals great by starting the second game. The Cubs presented Williams with a Chrysler Imperial automobile, a fishing boat, a motor, a pool table, a washer and dryer, and a watch.

"I got emotionally upset up there when they were presenting me everything," Williams said. "The standing ovations had me thinking back to my rookie year. It really shook me up."

He was toasted in Cooperstown in 1987 when Williams was inducted into the Hall of Fame. In his speech, he encouraged major league owners to "make a difference" and not look at the color of a man's skin but consider his talent, knowledge, and leadership to be manager.

"If this is the land of opportunity, then let it be truly a land of opportunity for all," Williams said.

The Cubs honored Williams again in 2010 by unveiling a statue of the outfielder outside Wrigley Field. When Cubs general manager Jim Hendry announced the tribute, he became choked up because of the impact Williams had on him as a special advisor.

"It couldn't happen to a better guy," Hendry said.

Or a better hitter. Some hitters need to analyze their swings on video, but sometimes all they need is a good pair of eyes.

"It's still the same game," Schwarber said, comparing his playing days to Williams'. "The pitcher is still standing away 60 feet 6 inches. People want to say the game has changed a lot, and trust me there are things that have changed in the game since Billy played, but it's still the same basics of the game and you still want to have a good solid approach and foundation when you're walking up to the plate, because if you don't have that, you're not going to have any success.

"Any time you can pick a guy's brain who has been there, done it at a high level of what he did, it can only help you down the line."

So Kyle Schwarber listened to Billy Williams, who listened to Rogers Hornsby.

"We used to talk all the time," Williams said of Hornsby. "I remember, he'd get in the batting cage—he was about 50 or 60 years old. He'd show me his stance—he stood way back in the batter's box. He'd stride into the plate. He said he saw the ball a little longer than the average guy. He'd hit the ball all over the field.

"I wish I could've gotten some balls signed by him."

23

NO-HITTER ROUNDUP

Sam Jones was the first Black pitcher to throw a no-hitter in the big leagues. Don Cardwell was the first pitcher to throw a no-no in his first game with a team. Jake Arrieta was the first to accomplish the feat then show up at his postgame news conference wearing a onesie. And Carlos Zambrano was first to throw a no-hitter at a neutral site.

The Cubs pitchers who have thrown no-hitters are a unique group. Let's start with Big Z.

In 2008, the Cubs were scheduled to play the Astros at Minute Maid Park, but those games had to be moved because of Hurricane Ike, which had damaged parts of Houston. (Reliant Stadium, home of the NFL Texans, lost some of its roof.) Major League Baseball determined the games would be played September 14–15 at Miller Park in Milwaukee.

Zambrano would start September 14, which would be his first game after missing two outings because of tendinitis in his right shoulder. The Astros weren't too pleased, because even though they were the "home" team, Miller Park had been turned into "Wrigley Field North" by thousands of Cubs fans who regularly made the drive to Milwaukee for normal games against the Brewers. A crowd of 23,441 attended the first game of the series—and saw history.

Zambrano retired the side in order in the first three innings, then walked Michael Bourn in the fourth and hit Hunter Pence with a pitch in the fifth. Those turned out to be the only base runners against him. Zambrano struck out 10, including Darin Erstad to end the game and record his only career no-hitter.

"Dominating stuff from pitch one until the end," Cubs right fielder Mark De Rosa said. "It's special to be a part of stuff like that."

The 5–0 victory was the Cubs' first no-no since Milt Pappas threw one September 2, 1972, which ended the longest drought by any team to have already had a no-hitter.

Zambrano had come close on August 22, 2003, against the Diamondbacks, but Shea Hillenbrand ended that bid with a single with two outs in the eighth inning.

"When I saw the stuff tonight, I said, 'This is kind of eerie,'" said Cubs pitching coach Larry Rothschild, who also watched that near-no-no in Phoenix. "It's a dome [like Arizona], and the roof was closed there. It was closed tonight. And we were in the first base dugout there, too. It was kind of strange. I said, 'I don't know what's going to happen here, but if he maintains his stuff, he's got a chance.'"

The final out in Milwaukee brought a happy roar, of course, from the theoretically neutral Miller Park crowd.

"The Cubs are a tough team, no matter where you play them," Houston's Lance Berkman said. "But we certainly would like to get them on more of a neutral field than in front of their home fans."

Cardwell most likely felt like a visitor at Wrigley Field on May 15, 1960, when he made his Cubs debut just two days after being acquired from the Phillies with Ed Bouchee for Tony Taylor and Cal Neeman.

"Being traded makes you feel as if you aren't wanted," Cardwell said after the deal.

The Cubs were happy they got him. In the second game of a doubleheader, Cardwell no-hit the Cardinals, allowing one base runner, Alex Grammas, who walked with one out in the first. The right-hander became the first pitcher in major league history to throw a no-no in his first game after being traded and did so in an efficient 1 hour 46 minutes.

When he met with reporters after the 4–0 win, Cardwell's gear was still packed in a Phillies bag next to his locker.

"A couple of kids back of the dugout kept telling me how many men I had retired in a row and how many I had to go," Cardwell told the *Chicago Tribune*.

He needed some help in the ninth: right fielder George Altman caught Carl Sawatski's line drive at the wall for the first out, and Walt "Moose" Moryn grabbed Joe Cunningham's sinking line drive in left to end the game.

Cardwell received a $2,000 bonus for the feat, which boosted his salary to $10,000.

"It was great, and I have thoroughly enjoyed it," Cardwell said. "All my career, people have come up to me and said, 'Did you pitch a no-hitter?' and I can say, 'Yes, yes I did.'"

Arrieta can say that twice—but it was the first one that was especially...unusual.

The Cubs had acquired the right-hander from the Orioles in July 2013 in a trade that included Pedro Strop. Arrieta needed some time in the minor leagues to get back on track, and in 2015, everything clicked. On August 30, 2015, the Cubs were finishing a West Coast trip in Los Angeles, a junket that had not gone well; they were 1–4 on the trip heading into the getaway Sunday-night game against the Dodgers.

The Cubs gave Arrieta a 2–0 lead thanks to Kris Bryant's home run with Chris Denorfia (walk) aboard the first inning. The Cubs didn't score again despite knocking out 13 hits in the game—but it didn't matter: Arrieta was masterful, striking out 12 and walking one.

Manager Joe Maddon had insisted players wear pajamas for the long flight back to Chicago, and most of them had found extra large-sized onesies. When Arrieta walked into the room to discuss his no-hitter, he was wearing one decorated with mustaches.

"He has that kind of stuff nightly—it's really crazy," Maddon said, referring to the pitching, not the pajamas. "The ball looks like a Wiffle ball from the side. You can see the break on the slider and the cutter and the curveball. Right now, he's pitching on another level. And he deserves it."

The Cubs had called that week "Cy Young Week" because they had to face top pitchers Corey Kluber, Jake Peavy, and Clayton Kershaw as well as World Series MVP Madison Bumgarner. (Alex Wood, who would go 16–3 two years later, started the finale for the Dodgers.)

"Why not have him conclude [Cy Young Week]?" Maddon said. "Maybe it's a harbinger."

Maddon was prescient. Arrieta won 22 games in 2015 and posted a 1.77 ERA in 33 starts to win the year's top pitching honor.

"Toothpick" Sam Jones had bounced around the rapidly fading Negro Leagues before signing with the Cleveland Indians organization in 1949 and playing in their system for years, then landed with the Cubs in 1955. His curveball was legendary; his control, occasional. With Triple-A San Diego, a Cleveland affiliate, in 1951 he fanned 246 in 267 innings—and walked 175.

Still, "If you'd pick one man in advance who might throw a no-hitter it would have to be Jones," said Cubs coach Bob Scheffing. "That's because he has such tremendous stuff."

On May 12, 1955, Jones no-hit the Pirates at Wrigley Field, chewing on a toothpick the entire time. He got into trouble in the ninth when he walked the bases loaded with nobody out. Cubs manager Stan Hack apparently considered pulling the pitcher, but catcher Clyde McCullough convinced Hack that Jones was okay—and the right-hander struck out Dick Groat, Roberto Clemente, and Frank Thomas (not the Hall of Famer) on 12 pitches to end the game and preserve the no-hitter.

"When Jones saw me walking toward the mound in the ninth inning after he had walked the first three, his jaw dropped and he gave me a hangdog expression," Hack told the *Chicago Tribune*. "If it hadn't been such a tight moment, I'd have busted out laughing."

Jones, who was one of three Black players in the Cubs' lineup that day along with shortstop Ernie Banks and second baseman Gene Baker (who had broken their color line just two years earlier), said Satchel Paige taught him how to throw the curveball. The no-hitter was one of the few highlights for Jones, who won 14 games but finished with 20 losses, most in the league that season.

"I didn't know I was working on a no-hitter until I came out in the ninth," Jones said. "Every time I pitched, the fans yelled. I finally looked at the scoreboard, and then I knew what all the shouting was about."

And lest we forget: the Cubs' Hippo Vaughn had a no-hitter for nine innings on a cold and blustery May 2, 1917, against the Reds' Fred Toney, who also had not given up a hit. It's the only time in major league history that two pitchers both had no-hitters over nine. The Reds broke through with one out in the 10th when Larry Kopf singled between second baseman Larry Doyle and first baseman Fred Merkle. One out later, Jim Thorpe hit a grounder in front of the plate that Vaughn tried to scoop up and toss to catcher Art Wilson, but Kopf was safe. Toney got his no-hitter; Vaughn had to settle for a two-hit loss. The final, in 10 innings: 1–0, in front of 3,500 in Weeghman Park.

24

HACK WILSON

I n 1930, Hack Wilson was the best hitter in baseball. The Cubs outfielder led the major leagues with 56 home runs and initially 190 RBIs (more on that number later). It marked the fifth straight season he'd driven in more than 100 runs. Wilson was at the top of his career. The Cubs rewarded him with a salary of $40,000—matching the great Rogers Hornsby's.

But his success was short-lived and a lesson for future ballplayers.

There are a couple theories on how Lewis Robert Wilson got his nickname. Some said with nearly 200 pounds packed onto a 5'6" frame, he looked like pro wrestler George Hackenschmidt. Others felt he resembled Hack Miller, the son of a circus strongman and a former Cubs outfielder.

The Cubs had acquired Wilson from the Giants in 1925 because of an administrative mistake. After batting .239, he was left unprotected on the Toledo roster, and the Cubs were able to draft the outfielder for $5,000.

In 1930, Joe McCarthy was the Cubs' manager, and his lineup featured Woody English and Kiki Cuyler batting ahead of Wilson. English posted a .430 on-base percentage; Cuyler had a .428 OBP. They gave Wilson plenty of opportunities to drive in runs. It also helped that the ball was jumping that season—nine of the 16 major league teams batted over .300, and the NL as a whole hit .303.

In early August, Wilson boasted to Chicago reporters that he would set a new home run record. He delivered—easily passing the Phillies' Chuck Klein, who set a league mark with 43 a year earlier—although Wilson had to avoid lemons and other projectiles thrown by fans bitter about his outfield play during the 1929 World Series.

A quick flashback: the Cubs had an 8–0 lead over the Philadelphia Athletics after six innings in Game 4 of the '29 World Series. A win, and the Cubs would have evened the series at two wins apiece. But the A's scored 10 runs in the seventh, including three on a fluke inside-the-park home run by Mule Haas. Wilson, who was playing center field, had misplayed Bing Miller's fly ball earlier that inning, and then lost Haas' fly ball in the sun.

The A's won, and clinched the series with a 3–2 win in Game 5.

Wilson's miscues prompted someone to pen new lyrics to "My Old Kentucky Home," beginning with: "The sun shone bright into poor Hack Wilson's eyes..."

"You're looking at a man who is more famous for one play he didn't make than all the home runs he ever hit," Wilson told the *Washington Post*'s Shirley Povich. "I hit 56 home runs with the Cubs the next year to set a new National League record. I led the league in homers for three years. I hit more than 230 home runs, but people point me out as the fellow who didn't catch that pop fly in one of my 1,200 big league games."

The Baseball Writers Association of America was impressed with what Wilson did in 1930, and a BBWAA committee voted to name him Most Valuable Player. But the selection was unofficial because the NL had abandoned its custom of picking an MVP that year.

Armed with the new contract, Wilson enjoyed his success. He drank heavily but insisted he never played drunk.

"Hungover, yes; drunk, no," Wilson said.

He was 20 pounds overweight when he arrived for spring training in 1931. McCarthy (who also was known to enjoy a beverage from time to time) had protected Wilson, but with McCarthy gone to the Yankees, the Cubs had a new manager in Hornsby, who wasn't as permissive. In early September, Wilson was suspended because of the "failure to observe training rules" as issued by Hornsby. The September 8, 1931, *Chicago Tribune* wrote that Wilson also had "remarked within hearing of several teammates that all the officials of the Cubs could go where there are no snowballs."

"Wilson probably has done more to lend color and atmosphere to baseball in Chicago than any other player of the last decade," wrote the *Chicago Tribune*'s Arch Ward in September 1931. "Thousands have been thrilled by his long drives, his timely wallops, his fight, and his leadership. His employers appreciated his efforts. He was rewarded with one of the highest salaries in baseball.

"There is nothing ordinary about Wilson. He's one of those home run or nothing fellows. So it is not altogether surprising that he is passing out only a few moments after reaching the peak of his fame. He always is doing the unusual."

In December 1931, Wilson was traded to Brooklyn and would play three more seasons but fail to match what he did in 1930.

A framed copy of a newspaper article titled HACK'S LAST WARNING used to be posted on a wall of the Cubs' home clubhouse before it was renovated in 2016. In it, Wilson says:

"Talent isn't enough. You need common sense and good advice. If anyone tries to tell you different, tell them the story of Hack Wilson.

"There are kids in and out of baseball who think because they have talent they have the world by the tail. It isn't so. Kids, don't be too big to accept advice. Don't let what happened to me happen to you."

Those quotes were from an interview Wilson did in 1948. About a week later, he fell in his apartment and died a few days after that. He was 48 years old.

His 56 home runs stood as the NL single-season record until 1998, when both Mark McGwire (70) and Sammy Sosa (66) topped it.

Fifty-one years after his death, Wilson drove in another run.

James Braswell, a student at Northwestern University, was researching the record for most consecutive games with an RBI and discovered a discrepancy. He sent a note to the Sporting News:

Gentlemen:
I believe if you check Hack Wilson's record from July 24 thru August 5, inclusive, of 1930, you will find Wilson knocked in at least one run in 11 consecutive games, and should be listed in your Baseball Record Book—along with Mel Ott—as the co-holder of this N.L. record.

The Sporting News forwarded the note to baseball Hall of Fame historian Cliff Kachline, and he enlisted SABR member Bob Soderman and archivist Paul McFarlane to review box scores and newspaper accounts from the *Chicago Tribune*, *Chicago Daily News*, *Chicago Daily Times*, and *Chicago Herald-Examiner*.

What they discovered was Charlie Grimm had been credited with two RBIs in the third inning of the second game of a doubleheader on

July 28 against the Reds—but Wilson had actually driven in Cuyler and should have been credited with an RBI. Kachline and Co. presented their research to baseball historians Jerome Holtzman, Seymour Siwoff, and Peter Hirdt of the Elias Sports Bureau and Rich Levin of the commissioner's office. MLB officially announced the change in June 1999.

"We're not the kind of people who like to make changes," Siwoff said, "but this was obvious. There was no way not to change it, because all the evidence was there."

Wilson's 191 RBIs in a single season is a baseball record that is revered in the same way as Joe DiMaggio's 56-game hitting streak, or Cal Ripken Jr.'s 2,632 consecutive games played streak, or Cy Young's 511 career wins.

Hopefully, Hack Wilson was able to celebrate.

25

JACK BRICKHOUSE

For generations of Cubs fans, the voice (aside from their parents') that defined their childhoods was Jack Brickhouse's. As soon as they got home from school and turned on WGN-TV to catch the last couple of innings, Brickhouse was there, enthusiastic and optimistic, no matter what was happening in the game.

"[Jack Rosenberg] would always say, and still does, that Jack never saw the Cubs lose," said Bob Vorwald, WGN-TV's director of production.

But the Cubs did lose often during Brickhouse's long tenure in the broadcast booth (1948–81) and posted a winning record in only seven of those 34 seasons before Brickhouse stepped aside for Harry Caray.

"Ernie [Banks] always said he got his optimism from Jack, but between the two of them they shaped an entire generation and, really, going forward, the fact that Cub fans were always optimistic, even though our team sucked," Vorwald said. "To me that all came out of Ernie and Jack, and Ernie said he got it from Jack."

Brickhouse was the one who said, "Any team can have a bad century." And he did it with a smile.

He's recognized at Wrigley Field by his trademark "hey-hey" adorning the two foul poles. Brickhouse first said that after one of Hank Sauer's home runs at Wrigley Field in 1949. The WGN-TV crew added a graphic of his exclamation at the bottom of the screen. Brickhouse saw it, everyone laughed, and they decided to keep it whenever a Cubs player hit a home run.

"He always looked for the positives," Banks told the *Chicago Tribune*. "He always said positive things about people."

Born in Peoria, Illinois, Brickhouse worked at a radio station there when he was 18 years old. In 1940, he was hired by WGN Radio to broadcast the Cubs and White Sox games, and he became the main voice for both teams when WGN-TV began broadcasting in 1948. (The Sox and the station split after the 1967 season; Brickhouse stayed with WGN-TV and the Cubs.)

"He was a remarkable human being," said Rosenberg, who was the sports editor for WGN Radio and WGN-TV from 1954 to '94. "It didn't matter whether it was the first inning or the eighth inning. The enthusiasm was always the same."

Brickhouse knew his audience.

"Sociability," Rosenberg said of Brickhouse's approach. "WGN had a reputation as a family station, and a lot of it was Jack."

Brickhouse wasn't just Mr. Baseball in Chicago. He also was the voice for Chicago Bears football on WGN Radio for 24 years and called play-by-play for some Chicago Bulls basketball games from 1966 to '73 as well. He was paired with Vin Scully for the 1959 White Sox–Dodgers World Series (an era when NBC featured local teams' announcers for the Series), and partnered with Mel Allen for the 1952 Rose Bowl (Illinois vs. Stanford) and with Chris Schenkel for NFL championship games in 1956 and '63, both featuring the Bears.

Every time you see the video of Ernie Banks' 500th career home run, it's Brickhouse's jubilant voice with the call.

"There's a fly ball, deep to left, back, back—hey-hey! He did it! Ernie Banks got number 500! The ball tossed to the bullpen, everybody on your feet—this is it! Wheee!"

Brickhouse had Cubs fans on the edge of their seats on May 15, 1960, when Don Cardwell was trying to get the last out of a no-hitter against the Cardinals. It was Cardwell's Cubs debut. The batter was Joe Cunningham, the Cubs' left fielder Walt "Moose" Moryn:

"Watch it now—hit on a line to left. Come on, Moose! He caught it! Moryn made a fabulous catch! It's a no-hitter for Cardwell! What a catch that Moryn made. What a catch he made."

Working most games without an analyst (sidekicks then generally just filled in for an inning or two and did commercials), Brickhouse let the images on the TV screen tell the story and kept his descriptions to a minimum. He received the Ford C. Frick Award from the Baseball Hall of Fame in 1983.

"I've telecast more than 4,800 Cub games," Brickhouse told the *Chicago Tribune*'s David Condon in 1981. "I don't see how anyone else can ever come close. Yet after all the years, I'm more enthusiastic about baseball than as a teenager broadcasting Peoria's Three-I League games.

WRIGLEY 1937

About those vines...

When Wrigley Field was first built—and it was known as Weeghman Park at the time—it was a single-deck ballpark that had a seating capacity of 14,000. There was no ivy on the outfield walls, because those bleacher walls didn't exist. The scoreboard? It was at ground level in center field.

In 1937, owner Philip K. Wrigley announced the addition of new bleachers, which the *Chicago Tribune* described as a chance to give "bargain seeking fans a larger number of seats and more comfortable seats. But, if the truth were known, the desire for scenic distinction probably was more of an incentive than the desire to spring the capacity of the field."

The ambience of the ballpark was important. Wrigley had tracked the attendance and discovered that if the Cubs weren't doing well, fewer people attended—not exactly a startling discovery. But if he couldn't guarantee a winner, how could he entice fans to come to games?

Beautiful Wrigley Field.

The best asset Wrigley had was the ballpark, and he wanted to promote Wrigley Field as the main attraction, which meant it had to be family-friendly, clean, and freshly painted, and provide good food. Ticket-takers must be polite and ushers were told to escort fans to their seats. Announcers were to say "Beautiful Wrigley Field" as often as possible.

Wrigley hired architectural firm Holabird & Root, founded in 1880 and designers of buildings including Chicago's Soldier Field, Board of Trade Building, and Palmer House Hotel, to design the bleachers and the hand-operated scoreboard (both received landmark status in 2004). Work on the new left and center field bleachers began on July 9, 1937, the start of a 15-day road trip by the Cubs.

Perry Stadium in Indianapolis had ivy-covered walls and was part of the inspiration for Wrigley Field's greenery. Wrigley also wanted trees planted in containers atop risers alongside the center field bleachers, so Chinese elms were installed in boxes—but the Chicago wind kept knocking them over. After several attempts and much investment, that idea was scrapped.

The plan had been to plant ivy at the end of the 1937 season after the bleacher construction was completed. But Wrigley had invited some people to see a game in September and expected to see the outfield walls covered in greenery. Trouble is, ivy can't grow that fast.

Bill Veeck Jr., later known for his promotions as owner of the St. Louis Browns, Cleveland Indians, and (twice) the White Sox, was working in the Cubs' front office in 1937, as did his father before him. He wrote in his autobiography that he contacted a nursery and overnight, he and workers planted 350 Japanese bittersweet plants at the base of the outfield wall.

That nursery was run by Elmer Clavey and his sons, who were second- and third-generation in the horticulture business. (Clavey's nursery took care of the landscaping at Wrigley's other properties.) They mixed in 200 Boston ivy plants with the bittersweet, knowing they would eventually grow out and thicken the wall covering. And they did.

Baseball historian Ed Hartig notes the Claveys had more to do with the ivy than Veeck, and that it was a source of pride for the Clavey family that it was involved with the Wrigley Field ivy. Though the family is no longer in the business, there's still a Clavey nursery in Harvard, Illinois, northwest of Chicago.

No Clavey is mentioned in Veeck's book. And there's no mention of Veeck in the nursery.

Now, about that iconic scoreboard...

The center field scoreboard also was built in 1937. Rather than copy the ones at the other major league ballparks, Wrigley was hoping for something unique. Holabird & Root came up with the design, creating a 27-foot-wide and 75-foot-high structure. By elevating it in center field, it would be easier for fans to see.

According to Veeck's autobiography, an inventor proposed the system currently in use, suggesting the electromagnetic dots that designate the batter, balls and strikes, and outs. Veeck wrote that the inventor didn't finish the project and the Cubs had to hire some electricians to complete the job.

However, Veeck may have embellished that story as well. The father-son team of Halvor Peter Hubertz and Curtis Melvin Hubertz of Hubertz Electronics actually invented the scoreboard operating system and maintained it for another 30 years. The control panel to operate it is in the press box and about the size of an old typewriter.

"Nobody has been able to beat it in all these years," Curtis Hubertz told the Cubs *Vine Line* magazine about their invention. "The numbers are up there way before anyone can take their eyes off the field. It's fast, it's wonderful and we were very proud of it. Still are."

In 2007, Curtis Hubertz showed up at Wrigley Field with a large box packed with spare parts for the scoreboard that he'd found while cleaning his garage. He was able to present it to Rick Fuhs, known as "Quick Rick," who runs the control panel. Many celebrities who come to the press box to sing the seventh-inning stretch like to see how the scoreboard works.

Sometimes, Fuhs will let the visitor enter a number to appreciate how fast the information is relayed to the scoreboard.

So next time you admire the ivy-covered bleacher walls and that timeless (even with its clock) scoreboard, take a moment to toast the Claveys and the Hubertz family—and Mr. Wrigley—for their contributions to Beautiful Wrigley Field.

"And I've never regretted the reputation of being [a] superfan. Occasionally, I criticize, yet basically I'm the good guy. It's not my nature to nail people. Sure, lots of broadcasters are rough critics. They create controversy more to line their pockets than to safeguard the fans' interests."

Brickhouse ventured out of the ballparks and covered five national political conventions, recorded an audience with Pope Paul VI, and did one-on-one interviews with six presidents. He broadcast Golden Gloves boxing from Chicago Stadium and wrestling at Marigold Arena.

"If I'm anything, I'm versatile," Brickhouse said in August 1979. "There is nothing I have not done in this business."

John McDonough, the Cubs' marketing director from 1983 to 2007 (and later a Blackhawks executive), loved all the Brickhouseisms, like "for just a hot minute."

"I think you could make a case that Brickhouse was the greatest broadcaster in Chicago history, period," McDonough told the *Chicago Tribune*. "Be it political broadcaster, sports broadcaster...any category."

Brickhouse, Rosenberg, and WGN's longtime director Arne Harris connected the viewers to the team.

"They were just so conscious of the fact that they were doing the games for the Cub fans," Vorwald said. "They were so keenly aware of this responsibility that they were part of everybody's family. There was this idea that they owed something to the viewers.... That left its mark on me."

Brickhouse died in August 1998, five months after Harry Caray's passing. To many, Brickhouse is like the ivy on the outfield walls and the iconic scoreboard in center field.

"When I'm doing a ballgame," Brickhouse once said, "I'm there to provide a brief moment of joy and relief for those who might have had a bad day."

Or a bad century. But the joy he brought to those generations endures.

26

LEO DUROCHER

Cubs owner Philip Wrigley knew he needed to do something. His team had finished in the second division of the National League standings for 19 consecutive years after a 72–90 season in 1965. The two years of rotating "head coaches" hadn't changed anything. Home attendance languished. Who could get the Cubs back on track?

Leo Durocher?

The man known as The Lip had not managed since 1955. He'd skippered the Brooklyn Dodgers to an NL pennant in 1941 in his third season as a player/manager. In his fourth season managing the New York Giants in 1951, he led them to the pennant, and they won the World Series in '54.

But there also was some complicated history. In 1947, Durocher had been given a year's suspension from baseball for unspecified conduct and associations "detrimental to the game." His fiery temper often resulted in nasty feuds on the field with umpires. He said he never questioned an umpire's integrity, just his eyesight. He didn't want nice guys on his team but "scratching, diving, hungry ballplayers who come to kill you."

When Cubs general manager John Holland approached Durocher about the job, the former manager was living in Los Angeles, doing a radio show Monday through Friday and broadcasting the "Game of the Week" on Saturdays.

The Cubs introduced Durocher at Wrigley Field on October 25, 1965. There, he made it clear his title was manager, not head coach, to avoid any possible carryover from the Cubs' failed College of Coaches days.

"I was overwhelmed," Cubs third baseman Ron Santo told reporters about Durocher. "It's a great move. He's not used to handling a loser. He must think we're a first-division club, or he would not have taken the job."

Cubs fans had high hopes.

"You can't say that P.K. Wrigley didn't go for broke in this one," wrote *Chicago Tribune* columnist David Condon. "You have to admire him for it, too. The barbs of fans have been sharp. Praise would be almost a foreign sound to him. Yet Wrigley shrugged aside false pride to bring in a manager who could dictate a three-year contract, and who is more noisy, controversial and commanding than the Cubs front office actually would desire. Owner Philip Knight Wrigley has proved himself."

At his introductory news conference, Durocher also said he was not the manager of an eighth-place team. Well, in his first season, the 1966 Cubs finished 10th.

The noisy, controversial, and commanding Durocher was undeterred.

In 1967, the Cubs got off to a strong start and were tied for the National League lead on July 2 after a win over the Reds in front of a standing-room-only crowd of 40,464 at Wrigley Field. The headline of the *Chicago Tribune* sports section on July 3: CUBS WIN, 4–1; MOVE INTO FIRST PLACE! (My husband still has a copy of that newspaper.)

The Cubs finished third in '67 and again in '68. The 1969 Cubs have their own chapter in this book, but it's missing Durocher's getaway in late July.

On July 28, the Cubs manager told coach Pete Reiser that he was ill and left the game against the Dodgers in the third inning. However, instead of going home, Durocher flew out of Meigs Field, the city's downtown business airport, to Rhinelander, Wisconsin, to attend his stepson's party at a boys camp near Eagle River. Durocher planned on returning the next morning, but bad weather resulted in a choppy landing and the manager called in sick.

The Chicago media found out about Durocher's absence, and he had to meet with Wrigley. In his book *Nice Guys Finish Last*, Durocher said he told the Cubs owner—whom he always called "Mr. Wrigley"— that he did not have a legitimate excuse. Wrigley's response was to pardon his manager, although he asked for better communication in the future.

"If you wanted to visit your son for a week, it would have been all right with me," Wrigley told Durocher. "Just let me know where you are. Tell me what's going on so that when the newspapermen called, I could have said, 'I know where he's at. He called me and I told him to go ahead.'"

Why did Durocher go AWOL?

"Because every once in a while, Mr. Wrigley, I do stupid things. Haven't you read my life story?" Durocher said in his book. "I mean, didn't you find out anything about me before you hired me?"

Clubhouse tensions grew. Even Santo, so thrilled initially by the Durocher signing, had lost the love. "I grabbed Leo and had him around the neck," Santo said, in his autobiography, of a 1971 incident. The manager threatened to quit on the spot. Tempers cooled. Leo stayed.

But Durocher and the Cubs eventually did part ways in July 1972 per a mutual agreement.

"The only thing I regret is that I wasn't able to do better and win a pennant for the people here in Chicago and Mr. Wrigley," Durocher told reporters on July 29. "That has been my biggest disappointment."

The friction between Durocher and the players led to the manager's firing midway through the 1972 season. Wrigley said the change "will allow the players to find out for themselves if they are pennant contenders."

Randy Hundley, whom Durocher had traded for prior to his first year in Chicago, sent the manager a telegram that read:

```
Dear Skip, just a quick word of thanks
for the opportunity you gave me to play with
the Chicago Cubs. I'm sorry for the few
differences we had this season but appreciate
your patience with me at times when I just
couldn't seem to get things going.
```

It didn't take long for Durocher to find work again. On August 26 that year, he was hired to manage the Houston Astros. But after a contentious 1973 season in Houston—in which the Astros finished 82–80—he resigned.

The Lip would never manage again, but true to form, he stormed away a winner.

27

EL MAGO

Magicians say "abracadabra" when they are about to reveal the end of a trick. The word may or may not be from the Aramaic phrase "avra kehdabra," which means "I will create as I speak." But while etymologists argue about the source, those who love both words and baseball can agree to apply this modification to Javier Baez: "I will create as I play."

Baez's nickname is El Mago, which is Spanish for "The Magician." And anyone who watches the infielder, even for only one game, will likely see him do something that will hint at the supernatural.

It could be Baez at shortstop making a leaping catch of a 110-mph line drive by Bryce Harper, prompting amazement from the MVP outfielder.

"He's a stud," Harper said of Baez. "One of the best in the league at what he does in his craft. One of the best gloves, quickest hands, lot of fun to watch him play and see how he's progressed as a player. What a stud he is."

In that same game, Baez raced 130 feet to foul territory in left to grab a fly ball by pinch-hitter Adam Lind, drawing praise from manager Joe Maddon.

"I don't know who else makes that play," Maddon said.

Anyone who has watched Baez since he was drafted by the Cubs in 2011 says that a lot about this man.

It's impossible to pick one Baez moment—he adds to his personal highlight film almost every game—but Game 1 of the 2016 National League Championship Series against the Dodgers may be one of his best, even if he did make a mistake.

In the second inning, Baez blooped a hit to shallow center to drive in a run. Baez was aggressive on the base path and reached second base on the hit before moving up on a wild pitch. Jon Lester was at the plate and squared to bunt. The play called was a safety squeeze, but Baez broke early, taking a few steps toward home, which drew catcher Carlos Ruiz's throw. Baez was able to sprint home to beat the throw from third baseman Justin Turner. That opened a 3–0 lead, and the Cubs went

Jon Lester (left) and Javy Baez were named co-MVPs of the 2016 NLCS.
Baez's steal of home with Lester at the plate in Game 1 was a magical moment.
(Getty Images)

on to post an 8–4 victory. It was the team's first steal of home in the postseason since 1907.

"He's probably the most exciting player in baseball," Baez's then-teammate David Ross said after the game. "He's energetic and not scared of the moment. He stays true to who he is with base running and the flair he has. He doesn't shy away from the big moments. And for his instincts to steal home there and have the guts to do that, that should tell you a lot about Javy Baez. He's a fearless individual."

The Cubs would eliminate the Dodgers, and Baez would be named co–Most Valuable Player (with Lester) of the series.

How did Baez become such a daredevil? As a boy in Puerto Rico (the family moved to Florida when he was 13), he would play pickup baseball and basketball games, or ride his bike at breakneck speed.

"That's the way I grew up—I grew up on the streets, and not in a bad way on the streets," he told me. "My whole neighborhood had a lot of kids, and we used to play all day. We had a baseball field, we had a basketball court. We had so much fun."

He didn't have smooth, perfectly manicured fields, either. Balls would take quirky bounces off the dirt, and Baez learned to be quick with his hands. All Maddon, a free spirit himself, asked Baez to do was make the routine plays routinely.

"When the play requires craziness, you're there, you can do that," Maddon told him. "But the straight up ground ball, three-hopper to shortstop, come get the ball, play through it, make an accurate throw in a routine manner."

That message stuck.

Baez always knew he would play in the major leagues. That's one of the reasons the first tattoo he got was the MLB logo, which is inked on the back of his neck. His brothers, Rolando and Gadiel, have the same tattoo.

"[Rolando] didn't like tattoos," Javy said. "I started talking about getting one, and he came up with the idea and said 'Let's get a tattoo that means something to us.' Baseball has been in our lives forever."

Who will also forever be a part of Javier Baez's life is his sister, Noely, who died at the age of 21 in April 2015 from complications related to spina bifida.

"When my sister was born, doctors said she wouldn't last 20 minutes, that she wouldn't last from one room to another one," Baez told me.

Spina bifida is the most common permanently disabling birth defect in the U.S. and occurs when the spinal column does not close all the way. Noely could not walk, but she was very independent. When Baez got to the minor leagues, he outfitted a van so Noely could travel comfortably when his family visited him.

They didn't think of Noely as being different.

"When I was a little kid and I didn't understand her situation, yeah, I thought, 'Wow, we have a handicapped sister,' and it's hard for my mom," Baez said. "Once I started growing up and lived with her every day, I realized this is not hard for us. God gave us this miracle."

In 2018, Baez exploded offensively, hitting 34 home runs, driving in 111 runs and batting .290. He finished second in the Most Valuable Player voting to the Brewers' Christian Yelich, who batted .326 with comparable power numbers. The vote wasn't close—but Baez' defensive wizardry no doubt made voters think a little longer.

"He continues to amaze people with what he can do with the glove," said Jose Flores, who was the Cubs' minor league infield coordinator when Baez was coming up in the system. "They don't call him 'El Mago' for no reason. They call him 'The Magician' because he's special, really special."

28

KEN HOLTZMAN

Pitchers can be a little superstitious. Most have a pregame routine from which they don't like to deviate. Many prefer the comfort of having the same catcher behind the plate.

Ken Holtzman was 23 years old on August 19, 1969, when he started for the Cubs against the Braves at Wrigley Field. A St. Louis native who had attended the University of Illinois, Holtzman was facing a stacked lineup that included Felipe Alou (who led the league in hits the year before) and Hank Aaron (who was Hank Aaron).

Holtzman and catcher Bill Heath were cruising. The lefty had not given up a hit through seven innings and walked three. But with two outs in the top of the eighth, Heath was struck by a foul ball and broke his hand. Cubs manager Leo Durocher had no choice but to insert catcher Gene Oliver into the game.

That didn't bother Holtzman or throw him off his rhythm.

"I told Oliver, 'I'm going with fastballs all the way,'" said Holtzman, who was struggling with his curve. "He picked up where Heath left off."

Holtzman had already gotten an assist from nature in the seventh. The Cubs led 3–0, and Aaron hit a ball that looked as if it were going to end the no-hitter and the shutout. It was headed to the left field bleachers.

"I thought it was gone—even with the wind blowing in," Holtzman said.

WGN Radio's Vince Lloyd described the play.

"Billy Williams back to the bleachers, back to the corner...he grabbed it! Holy mackerel! That ball was ticketed for the bleachers and the wind moved it just away from the bleachers to the farthest corner of the wall out there, and Billy Williams staying with it, grabbed it right up against the vines!"

The crowd of 37,514 went crazy.

"If that happens, you think something's going on," Holtzman told me. "The gods must be looking in on the game. I've always said a no-hitter is just a well-pitched game with a lot of luck."

And it has nothing to do with superstitions. Oliver did fine behind the plate helping Holtzman record the final four outs and completing the first of his two career no-hitters.

"Today, Ken got his first no-hitter," Durocher told the *Tribune*'s David Condon and others after the game, "and gentlemen, this could very well be the beginning of another Koufax."

Aaron was pretty good, too. His fly ball in the seventh was well struck.

"I had pitched long enough to recognize the crack of the bat and the trajectory," Holtzman told Bob Vorwald in *Wrigley 100*. "When you throw a pitch like that, especially to a guy like Hank Aaron, OK, well now the score is 3–1."

After they retired, Aaron and Williams would relive the game and the catch when the two were together in Cooperstown, New York, for the annual Hall of Fame ceremony.

"Actually, when the ball was hit, my first reaction was to give up on it," Williams told Vorwald. "I happened to look around and I looked at the flag in center field and the wind was blowing in hard, so I gave it a try. Lo and behold, the ball started to come back in, because the ball was out of the ballpark. The only way I could catch the ball was to turn sideways."

Aaron had started his home run trot, thinking he'd connected despite the wind.

"I don't know why or how it stayed in the ballpark and came right in that little trough in Wrigley Field is where Billy ended up catching the ball," Aaron said. "I thought for sure that I hit a home run, and sure enough the wind blew it right back to Billy Williams."

Holtzman had to deal with Aaron one more time to complete his no-hitter.

"I had a 3–0 lead, there were two outs in the bottom of the ninth, the crowd is going absolutely crazy. I can't hear myself think, and Geno Oliver back there—he just wanted me to stay away from [Aaron]," Holtzman said. "He may get a hit but let's stay away from him, you know. I've still got to try and win the game.

"So I threw it as hard as I could and kept it away, and he hit a ground ball at [Glenn] Beckert," Holtzman said. "I turned around when he hit it—he didn't really hit it that hard, and Beck is shaking, he's nervous, boy. I don't think he wanted that ball hit to him."

But Beckert did make the play.

"He kind of double-clutched at it a couple of times," Holtzman said of his second baseman. "Finally he put his glove on it and knowing Beck, I was lucky he didn't throw it into the fourth row. He was only 20 feet away from Ernie [Banks], but he got it over there. You saw him kind of shake a little bit like he had nerves. He finally got enough and he threw it over to Ernie and that was the last I remember, because [Ron] Santo jumped on me, and I don't remember anything after that."

Less than two years later, Holtzman threw another no-hitter, shutting down the defending champion Reds 1–0 on June 3, 1971. The Cubs lefty retired the last 11 Reds in the game, striking out both Tommy Helms and Lee May in the ninth to complete the no-hitter, the first ever at Riverfront Stadium.

"I feel about the same way I did after the first one," Holtzman said after the game. "I'm kind of in a state of shock and I'm tired."

He was the first Cubs pitcher in the modern history of the team to throw two no-hitters. Some of the Cincinnati fans weren't interested in seeing history made.

"The fans in the first row behind our dugout wouldn't let me forget I had a no-hitter going tonight," Holtzman said. "I guess from the fourth inning on they would yell at me that I was going to lose my no-hitter."

He didn't.

And the catcher this time? With starter Randy Hundley missing most of the year with an injury—little-used Danny Breeden. In his first and last season as a Cub.

29

SWEET LOU

It did not take long for Lou Piniella to realize that managing the Cubs would be different from any other job he'd had.

During his first spring training with the team in 2007, a Japanese TV crew wanted to show Piniella's fiery temperament and asked the manager to stomp on a goat, which (symbolically, maybe) would put an end to the so-called Billy Goat Curse against the Cubs. To avoid any blood or problems with PETA, the TV crew subbed a small stuffed lamb instead. Piniella accommodated them with aplomb, kicking dirt and the toy with gusto.

The Cubs needed a kick after finishing last in the National League Central in 2006, which is why Piniella was hired. After playing 18 seasons, including 11 with the Yankees, Piniella had managed the Yankees, Reds, Mariners, and Devil Rays, leading Cincinnati to the World Series championship in 1990. He helped turn around the Mariners when he was in Seattle from 1993 to 2002 but couldn't do the same in Tampa Bay from 2003 to '05. After taking one year off to work in television, the Cubs named Piniella their manager in October 2006.

"I really feel strongly that Lou is the perfect guy for the task right now," Cubs general manager Jim Hendry said at the time.

When Piniella was hired, his past animated outbursts at umpires were highlighted in the Chicago newspapers' profiles. Many Cubs fans started a pool to predict when his first ejection would be. At that point in his career, he'd been tossed more than 50 times.

"I'm a fiery manager," Piniella said during his introductory news conference. "I'm basically a lot of fun to play for. I may be demanding, but that's part of the equation.

"I'm 63 years old, and once in a while I get into a little episode with an umpire, and I jump back and say, 'Why the hell did I do that?'"

What was more important to the Cubs was the team's performance on the field. Hendry went on a spending spree leading up to the 2007 season, re-signing Aramis Ramirez to a five-year, $75 million deal and acquiring free agents Alfonso Soriano (eight years, $136 million), Ted

Lilly (four years, $40 million), Jason Marquis (three years, $21 million), and Mark DeRosa (three years, $13 million).

"We won 66 ballgames [in 2006]. We darn sure better be aggressive," Hendry said.

"Long-suffering Cubs fans, we're going to win here," Piniella said. "And that's really the end of the story."

Piniella's first season in Chicago got off to a shaky start, and the Cubs were six games back in the division after a loss to the Marlins on May 30. First baseman Derrek Lee called a players-only meeting that day in an attempt to kick-start the team.

The next day did not go any better.

In the fifth inning against the Braves, Cubs starter Carlos Zambrano was charged with seven runs (one unearned) on 13 hits and catcher Michael Barrett made two misplays on the same play. Zambrano had enough and yelled at Barrett in the dugout.

"I was just telling him, 'Are you out of your mind?'" Zambrano said later.

They got into a fight and had to be separated. Both went into the clubhouse and got into another fight.

"It's frustrating for everybody," Piniella said. "These things shouldn't happen among teammates. Go fight the other team if you have to."

Barrett needed six stitches in his lip. Neither player wanted to talk about the clubhouse fracas.

"Whatever happens in Vegas stays in Vegas," Zambrano said.

Whomever had June 2, 2007, in the Piniella ejection pool won. In the eighth inning, the Cubs' Angel Pagan doubled and then tried to advance to third when the ball got away from Braves catcher Jarrod Saltalamacchia. Pagan was called out. Piniella disagreed. The crowd of 40,290 at Wrigley Field finally saw the combustible Lou Piniella they'd heard about.

The Cubs manager kicked the dirt, booted his cap, and went nose-to-nose with third-base umpire Mark Wegner, yelling his objections and his frustrations before he was ejected. Crew chief Bruce Froemming said it was a "terrible display of disrespect." The fans loved it.

The Cubs dropped that game 5–3 for their sixth straight loss. Asked about his outburst: "I think it was time," Piniella said. "But I really did think the guy was safe."

It was perfect timing for the Cubs, who went 63–46 after that point to win the NL Central, becoming the first team in the division to go from worst to first.

"When Lou got ejected," Cubs reliever Will Ohman said, "I think that was 25 guys on the team, coaching staff, and everybody who is a Cubs fan exploding at one moment, saying, 'We are ticked. This is not the way we planned this.' I thought that was a release, a tension release."

"It might have been that [the season] already was starting to change—you don't know," Piniella said.

Whatever propelled the Cubs didn't continue into the postseason, and they were swept by the Diamondbacks in the NL Division Series.

With Game 1 tied at 1 after six innings, Piniella pulled starter Carlos Zambrano after 85 pitches. He wanted to be careful with Zambrano's pitch count because the right-hander might be needed for Game 4. Reliever Carlos Marmol served up a leadoff home run to Mark Reynolds in the seventh, and the D-backs won 3–1.

"I took a shot. It didn't work. Period. End of the story," Piniella said. There would be no Game 4.

Lilly started Game 2 and gave up a three-run homer to rookie outfielder Chris Young in the second, prompting the pitcher to fling his glove to the ground on the mound. In Game 3, Young smacked the first pitch from Cubs starter Rich Hill for another homer and the D-backs won 5–1. It was over quickly.

"This is just the start, fellas," Piniella said. "We're going to get better with this."

The Cubs reached the playoffs again in 2008 but were swept again in the NLDS, this time by the Dodgers. They finished second the next year but struggled at the start of the 2010 season. In July, Piniella announced he would retire at the end of the season to take care of his mother, Margaret, who was in poor health. But her condition worsened, and on August 22, Piniella made the surprise announcement that he was headed home to Tampa, Florida, after the game.

Never one to hide his emotions, Piniella cried when he told the players he was leaving and once more after exchanging lineup cards at home plate that day with the Braves' Bobby Cox. The Wrigley Field crowd chanted "Lou, Lou" whenever he made a pitching change.

"He's given his life to the game," Cubs catcher Koyie Hill said. "I think the 25 guys in this room appreciate everything he's done for us and know [home] is where he should be."

And after nearly 50 years in baseball, Lou Piniella took off his uniform for the last time.

30

DALLAS GREEN

Imagine being a young baseball fan and you write the general manager of your favorite team with some ideas about the roster. You like Leon Durham and would like to see the struggling outfielder get more playing time.

Rick Hahn, who at 11 was not yet general manager of the White Sox, was growing up a Cubs fan in suburban Winnetka and sent such a suggestion in a letter to Dallas Green, who at 48 was in his first season as the Cubs' GM.

"I think the first thing I wrote, I had some trade ideas for Bill Buckner because I wanted to make room for Leon Durham," Hahn told me about a letter he sent in September 1982. "Dallas was kind enough to write me back and say something to the effect of, 'We feel we're going to get to a good solution on the Buckner situation—keep rooting.' He'd clearly read it. It was a nice short note.

"Then I wrote him back two more times," Hahn said. "One time I had lineup ideas and the other was trade ideas. He wrote back each time. It was a short little note but very kind. The fact he acknowledged it as a 10-, 11-year-old fan, it means the world to you. I haven't forgotten that."

One of Green's letters to Hahn stated:

> Thanks for your recent letter regarding your thoughts on our players and suggested trades.
>
> During the off-season we will make some changes to improve the Cubs for 1983. We will work hard to develop a team our fans will be proud to support.
>
> Keep rooting!
> Sincerely,
> Dallas Green

Fast forward to 2002: Hahn joined the White Sox that year and was named the team's general manager in 2013. And he has received letters from fans.

"As a means of trying to pay forward Dallas' kindness to me, I do respond to them," Hahn said. "If it's some guy in his thirties who's just pissed off, no, he doesn't get a letter. But if it's clearly some kid, I feel some cosmic obligation to return the kindness that Dallas showed to me."

Green had plenty to do regarding the Cubs besides correspondence. He inherited a team that hadn't been to the postseason in 36 years, that had posted a plus-.500 record just eight times in that span, that had a weak farm system—and that wasn't allowed to play night games in its home ballpark.

"Going to the Chicago Cubs was a tremendous experience," Green said. "They were the dregs of the National League. They weren't respected at all by their peers, they had a terrible team and a terrible working relationship with the fans. We worked hard to turn it around, so I was proud of what we did there."

Green had pitched for eight seasons and managed in the major leagues, guiding the 1980 Phillies to that team's first-ever World Series championship. Why leave the Phillies for the Cubs?

"This is the top of my career," Green told the *Chicago Tribune*'s Skip Myslenski in February 1982. "I'm not going to own a club, I'm certainly not going to be commissioner of baseball, so to become a general manager is what I'm going to be—and there's nothing more exciting than taking a club that needs some help, giving it that help, and watching it come along. Hopefully, that will happen."

He made his presence felt immediately with the Cubs, beginning with the slogan, "Building a New Tradition."

"I went to Chicago with guns blazing and big mouth blazing about what I intended to do," Green said. "When I first went there, everybody talked about time frames. I told them I have no time frames. I want results rather quickly, and I want to make things happen quickly."

Green did lean on his Phillies connections, bringing manager Lee Elia, coach John Vukovich, farm director Gordon Goldsberry, and scout Hugh Alexander with him to the Cubs.

"He had a vision and knew what was going to happen," said Dave Martinez, who was drafted by the Cubs in 1983. "He was trying to build an organization [from] within, and he really did that."

Green also acquired a few Phillies players in trades, including Keith Moreland, Dickie Noles, Larry Bowa, Ryne Sandberg, Bob Dernier, and Gary Matthews.

"We had been raised in Philadelphia to differentiate guys who could play first-division, championship baseball versus second-division kind of guys," Green told me. "I had been around the so-called gamers as a result of my 1980 and '81 managing business with Philadelphia.

"Larry Bowa is the kind of guy I call a 'gamer.' Ryne Sandberg, I knew from the minor leagues. I knew he had the heart, and pride, and gamesmanship to make himself a player and be a good player. Those kinds of people we felt we had to bring to Chicago because, to be honest with you, we couldn't find them anywhere in Chicago or throughout their minor league system."

The Cubs finished fifth in both 1982 and '83. But in May '84, Green traded Buckner to the Red Sox (opening first base for Durham, a better position for him, and no doubt thrilling the young Rick Hahn) for Dennis Eckersley. Then he made his biggest move three weeks later when he orchestrated a seven-player deal with the Indians, acquiring pitcher Rick Sutcliffe for, among others, a very raw Joe Carter.

Sutcliffe was 4–5 with a 5.15 ERA in 15 starts with the Indians but went 16–1 with a 2.69 ERA in 20 starts with the Cubs to help them win the National League East title and secure their first trip to the postseason since 1945. Sutcliffe won the Cy Young Award that year, and Sandberg, who batted .314 with 19 homers and 84 RBIs, was named Most Valuable Player. (Carter, of course, two years later would blossom into a star at Cleveland and make his own postseason history later with the Blue Jays—against the Phillies—but not in this chapter.)

Green and Goldsberry boosted the Cubs' farm system by drafting players such as Shawon Dunston in the first round in 1982, Greg Maddux and Jamie Moyer in 1984, Rafael Palmeiro in 1985, Joe Girardi in '86, and Mike Harkey in '87.

"Long-term improvement has to come from scouting, signing, and developing your own players," Green said. "Free agents are something we live with in this era of baseball, but I don't believe in buying a team."

Green also actively lobbied for lights at Wrigley Field so the Cubs could play night games, which angered some fans and rankled neighborhood activists. The Chicago city council and Mayor Harold Washington eventually did approve a change to an ordinance to allow night games, but the lights weren't turned on until 1988—months after Green had resigned from the organization over "philosophical differences."

For sure, Green left his mark.

"When you talk about a baseball man, that expression gets overused sometimes," said Jed Hoyer, who became Cubs general manager after the 2011 season and was promoted to president of baseball operations in 2020. "Dallas Green was the quintessential baseball man. He was a player, wins a World Series as a manager [with the Phillies], came close to winning one with the Cubs as an executive. Not a lot of people can say that."

Hahn never met Green, who died in March 2017. Green was 82. Hahn was 46.

"As a kid who was a crazy baseball fan, diehard baseball fan, the GM is sort of larger-than-life, almost a fictional character, and especially Dallas, given his bravado and presence and stature in the game," said Hahn. "The fact that he responded led me to continue to write. I feel a little bad because he probably felt, 'Enough, kid.'

"The baseball gods would not look kindly on me if I didn't at least take the same time to show the same kindness that Dallas showed to me."

31

KRIS BRYANT

It was November 2, 2016. Two out in the bottom of the 10th in Cleveland's Progressive Field, Cubs leading 8–7 in Game 7 of the World Series, their first since 1945, trying to win their first World Championship since 1908. Potential tying run taking a lead off first base. The Indians' Michael Martinez, who had taken Mike Montgomery's first pitch for a strike, bounced the next toward third.

The Cubs' third baseman that night had been named the College Player of the Year in 2013 and the Minor League Player of the Year the next season. In 2015, he was a unanimous pick as the National League Rookie of the Year. And in 2016, Kris Bryant would be voted the league's Most Valuable Player.

But *this* would be his moment.

Drift back a few years. Houston, surprising no one, had chosen pitcher Mark Appel at No. 1 in the 2013 draft. (By 2018, Appel would be out of baseball.) The Cubs, looking to fast-forward their rebuild under Theo Epstein, went for power—and in his junior year at the University of San Diego, Kris Bryant had led the nation's college players with 31 home runs and driven in 62 runs in 62 games.

(His father, Mike, had been a ninth-round pick by the Red Sox, and—despite being tutored a bit by Boston legend Ted Williams—lasted just two seasons in the minor leagues. But Dad would guide his son. "I'm just a better teacher than I am a hitter, I guess," he said.)

Bryant brought swagger along with his power.

"I obviously think I could play in the big leagues now," Bryant said after he was selected. "I have that type of confidence in myself, but, like I said, that's not my decision. I'll leave that up to the guys in charge."

That may sound cocky. It wasn't his intent.

"I think that in order to play this game, you have to have confidence in yourself," he told me months later when he was playing in the Arizona Fall League. "And if you don't have confidence that you can play in the big leagues, then you really shouldn't be playing baseball."

The Cubs tested Bryant in his first professional season. He passed the test. After playing 36 minor league games (and batting .336 with nine homers) in 2013, he was assigned to the Arizona Fall League, which is made up of players teams feel are close to the big leagues. He got some good karma when he was assigned No. 17, the same number his father had worn in the minors.

"He was never the dad who made me go out to the field and practice," Bryant said of his father, who had installed a batting cage at home. "It was me going out there asking him, 'Could you throw to me after work?'"

In 2014, Bryant belted 43 home runs and batted .325 combined at Double-A Tennessee and Triple-A Iowa.

Cubs manager Joe Maddon met Bryant for the first time in spring training in 2015 and was impressed.

"Of course, he's talented, great body, great power, wonderful arm, good third baseman, good outfield," Maddon said. "He knows he's good. There's also a humility about him, too."

But the Cubs front office insisted the third baseman still needed to work on his defense. There was speculation the decision was based more on service time—which can have a financial impact later—than on whether or not Bryant was ready. (By delaying Bryant's promotion 12 days into the season, the Cubs would gain an additional year of control before he would be eligible for free agency. He and the MLB Players Association would later file a grievance, which they lost in 2020.)

Whatever the reason, Bryant opened the 2015 season in the minors.

"He was straight up with me and looked me right in the eyeballs [saying he belonged in the big leagues], and I don't blame him," Maddon said of his conversation with Bryant regarding the demotion.

The demotion was brief. When starter third baseman Mike Olt was hit by a pitch on the right wrist on April 11, the Cubs needed a third baseman.

Iowa manager Marty Pevey gave Bryant the news rather nonchalantly. Bryant had just hit his third home run for the minor league team, and they were discussing foul poles. Bryant thought they should be a little taller.

"In the middle of that conversation, [Pevey] says, 'Oh, and you're going to the bigs tomorrow,'" Bryant said. "That's a pretty cool job. As a Triple-A manager, you can tell people their dreams are coming true."

His big-league debut on April 17, 2015, wasn't exactly the stuff dreams are made of. Bryant struck out in his first three at-bats against the Padres' James Shields, then grounded out in the seventh. He shrugged it off. After all, in his pro debut for Class A Boise in 2013, he'd struck out five times—and rebounded to bat .354.

"I've struck out plenty of times before," Bryant said. "I'm going to have a five-strikeout game again in my future. It's just baseball."

The next day, Bryant recorded his first and second big-league hits with an RBI single in the fifth inning and a single in the 11th in a win over the Padres. On May 9 in Milwaukee, he hit his first home run, a three-run shot in the third off Kyle Lohse. However, instead of returning to a celebratory dugout, Bryant's teammates had disappeared into the clubhouse as a joke, leaving the dugout empty.

Bryant recognized the prank and ran up the tunnel to find them.

"The funny part," Maddon said, "is he came after us to be congratulated."

The start of his major league career might have been delayed, but Bryant made up for that, setting franchise rookie records with 26 home runs, 99 RBIs, 62 extra-base hits, and 273 total bases. He was the unanimous pick as the NL Rookie of the Year.

There were no questions about whether Bryant was ready for the big leagues in his sophomore season. On April 21 in Cincinnati, he hit two home runs, including a grand slam, and drove in six runs to support Jake Arrieta's no-hitter against the Reds. Bryant topped that on June 27 at Great American Ball Park when he became the first player in MLB history to hit three home runs and two doubles in a game, again driving in six runs. On August 18, he collected five more hits, including two home runs, against the Brewers.

Bryant finished with 39 home runs and 102 RBIs to win the MVP award, while Anthony Rizzo hit 32 homers and drove in 109 runs (and finished fourth in the MVP voting). Rizzo gets his own chapter in this book, but it's worth mentioning here that the pair will forever be linked for completing the most famous groundout in Cubs history.

Bryant gloved Martinez's grounder on the third hop and fired a strike to Rizzo at first. And...

"Bryant makes the play! It's over! And the Cubs have finally won it all!"

32

MERKLE'S BONER

It was only a rookie mistake, but in 1908 it helped the Cubs get to the World Series.

Fred Merkle was 19 when he made his first start for the New York Giants on September 23, 1908, subbing for the regular first baseman, who was sidelined with lumbago. The Giants and Cubs were battling for the National League pennant, and with two outs in the ninth inning and the game tied at 1, Merkle was on first and Moose McCormick on third. Al Bridwell hit what should have been a game-winning RBI single, McCormick headed home, and fans ran onto the field at the Polo Grounds to celebrate what they thought was a 2–1 victory.

But Merkle didn't touch second base.

Instead, he ran into the clubhouse as Cubs center fielder Solly "Circus Solly" Hofman retrieved the baseball. In the confusion, Cubs second baseman Johnny Evers called to Hofman, Hofman threw the ball toward the infield, it reached Evers, and Evers stepped on second. Home-plate umpire Hank O'Day called Merkle out.

The run didn't count. Rule 4.09: "A run is not scored if the runner advances to home base during a play in which the third out is made...by any runner being forced out."

The game ended in a 1–1 tie.

"There have been some complicated plays in baseball," wrote Hall of Fame journalist Charles Dryden, "but we do not recall one just like this in a career of years of monkeying with the national pastime."

What helped the Cubs' argument was that a similar situation had happened in a game against the Pirates earlier that month, on September 4—and O'Day was the umpire then, too. That game was scoreless when Pittsburgh loaded the bases in the 10th inning. Chief Wilson singled to short center, driving in a run. But Warren Gill, who was on first base, only ran halfway to second and when he saw the ball land, he headed back to the dugout.

Evers saw Gill, who had been hit in the side by a pitch, break for the bench. The Cubs second baseman got the ball and stepped on second and tried to get O'Day's attention. However, the umpire had his back to the play. There was no instant replay in 1908. Game over.

"No more could [Fred] Clarke's run count as the play came up today but for the fact O'Day took it for granted the game was over when Wilson's hit landed safe just as Gill did," wrote I.E. Sanborn in the *Chicago Tribune*, "only Hank probably was in a hurry because he was hungry and Gill was hurrying away because he had sore slats."

The Cubs filed a protest of the September 4 game, which was later dropped after Merkle's misstep on September 23.

There's one more detail about the September 23 game that isn't often mentioned. Baseball historian Ed Hartig notes pitcher Joe McGinnity, who was the Giants' third-base coach in the game, interfered with the play. McGinnity grabbed at the ball when it was thrown in from center field, and Dryden wrote that it eventually "rolled among the spectators, who had swarmed upon the diamond like an army of starving potato bugs." As soon as the coach touched it, Merkle was considered out, and O'Day noted that in his report.

Giants manager John McGraw didn't blame the rookie for his base-running blunder, which Dryden dubbed a "bonehead" play (hence, Merkle's Boner).

In any case, the folks in Watertown, Wisconsin, don't think badly of their native son. In 2005, the city erected a monument to Merkle and named a ball field after him.

The plaque states:

THIS MEMORIAL IS DEDICATED TO THE LIFE OF FRED C. MERKLE. BORN IN WATERTOWN, WI, DEC. 20, 1888. HIS FATHER, ERNST MERKLE, WAS A SCHOOL TEACHER AT IMMANUEL LUTHERAN SCHOOL IN WATERTOWN AT THE TIME OF FRED'S BIRTH. FRED MADE HIS MAJOR LEAGUE DEBUT ON 9-21-1907. HIS OUTSTANDING TALENT, INTELLIGENCE AND DEDICATION TO THE GAME OF BASEBALL SPANNED 3 DECADES, HAVING BEEN A MEMBER OF 6 WORLD SERIES TEAMS: 1911, 1912, 1913, 1916, 1918 AND 1926. HE WAS A POTENT LINE-DRIVE HITTER, AGILE FIRST BASEMAN AND A SPEEDSTER ON THE BASE PATHS. HE PLAYED FOR THE NEW YORK GIANTS, BROOKLYN DODGERS, CHICAGO CUBS AND NEW YORK YANKEES.

Yes, Merkle played for the Cubs. The team purchased him from the Brooklyn Robins in 1917 for $3,500, and he played four seasons for them until he was released in January 1921.

The Cubs and Giants finished the 1908 regular season tied at 98–55—with many New York fans still blaming Merkle—and the two teams met October 8 to decide the NL champion. Chicago won 4–2 thanks to Mordecai Brown's 8⅓ innings in relief of starter Jack Pfiester and a four-run fourth inning sparked by Frank Chance's two-run double. The Cubs then beat the Tigers to win their second consecutive World Series championship—and last until 2016.

Postscript: 90 years after the Merkle play—to the day—the Cubs and Mets were tied for the NL wild card with three games remaining. On September 23, 1998, the Cubs were playing the Brewers and built a 7–0 lead, but Milwaukee pulled to within two runs in the bottom of the ninth. With the bases loaded and two outs, Geoff Jenkins hit a fly ball to left that Brant Brown dropped, prompting an "Oh, no!" from Cubs radio broadcaster Ron Santo that many fans can still hear. Three runs scored, and the Brewers won 8–7.

"You catch a thousand of those in batting practice every day," Brown said. "It was the 1,001st that I just happened to miss."

"Hopefully," Cubs first baseman Mark Grace said, "at the end of the season we can look back and laugh about this."

The Cubs—oh, yes—survived "Brown's Boner": they beat the Giants 5–3 in a one-game wild-card playoff to reach the postseason.

33

COLLEGE OF COACHES

A major league manager is criticized by fans and the media, and sometimes friends and family, and might not get much credit when his team is playing well. But he's rarely alone in the decision-making process. Baseball operations departments now employ analysts who break down statistics and tendencies, and that data helps the manager decide on who should lead off and which left-handed reliever is best in late innings. It's a group effort—but not like the one Cubs owner Philip Wrigley forced on the organization in 1961.

The Cubs, under managers Charlie Grimm and Lou Boudreau, finished in the second division of the National League in 1960 for the 14th consecutive season. Wrigley had enough and decided what worked in business would work in baseball: he named an eight-man coaching staff—a College of Coaches—that would rotate managing the team. Wrigley felt the players would benefit from being exposed to their varied approaches and expertise to the game. Coaches not with the major league team would be coaching in the minor leagues until rotating back to the big leagues, which Wrigley saw as an aid to developing young talent.

The original eight included Elvin Tappe, Charlie Grimm, Goldie Holt, Bobby Adams, Harry Craft, Verlon Walker, Rip Collins, and Vedie Himsl.

"Managers are expendable," Wrigley said. "I believe there should be relief managers just like relief pitchers."

Imagine having a new boss every week. Rules could change, dress codes might vary, and support-staff tasks most likely would be altered from boss to boss. That's what happened with the Chicago Cubs.

"It made headlines, I'll tell you that," Billy Williams, who lived through it, told me. "It didn't go well with a lot of people. It went all right with the coaches because a lot of guys got a chance to come to the big leagues. The only good thing I saw in that is you get four [coaches] at the major league level and they switch and send those guys to the minor leagues and they would see the kids who were at Double-A or Triple-A.

"It was something Mr. Wrigley wanted because he thought it would work—but I don't think it worked," Williams said.

Don Zimmer could tell it wasn't effective. The Cubs had acquired Zimmer from the Dodgers in April 1960, and the veteran infielder—and future manager—doubted the College of Coaches would function.

"First of all, when it's your time to manage for 10 days, what happens if you win 10 in a row?" Zimmer told me. "You'd stay, wouldn't you? They'd keep you. Well, how about the other guys? You think they're pulling for you? They're pulling against you so they get a chance."

Williams said the coaches had different thoughts on how to win a game.

"There's no single way to win," Williams said. "Everybody had their idea on how to do things."

In 1961, Ron Santo was a 21-year-old third baseman playing his second season with the Cubs. During games, one coach would have him move back on the field; another would tell Santo to come in. It was confusing.

"I think some of the coaches, they had a grudge against the other coaches," Williams said.

The changes didn't seem to bother Williams, who won the National League Rookie of the Year in 1961, batting .278 with 25 home runs and 86 RBIs. Were the rotating managers ever confusing for him?

"No, because I was on the field," Williams said. "I was just going to play baseball. That's what I did."

Four men took turns as the "manager" that season, resulting in a 64–90 record and seventh-place finish in the eight-team National League. The next season, the Cubs lost 103 games, winding up ninth place behind the expansion Houston Colt .45s and ahead only of the historically pathetic first-year New York Mets in the now 10-team league.

Wrigley finally stopped the revolving door and named Chicago native Bob Kennedy as the manager in 1963. The Cubs posted an 82–80 record, their first winning season since 1946.

"Right after he was named 'head coach,' a reporter asked him what he thought of the title," Terry Kennedy, Bob's son and a Cubs scout, told me. "He replied, 'I'm the manager, not a head coach.'"

But Kennedy's job title stayed "head coach" until he was fired during the 1965 season and replaced by Lou Klein, rotating in for a third time.

Wrigley finally junked the rotation system and hired Leo Durocher after that season.

"If no announcement has been made about what my title is, I'm making it here and now," Durocher told reporters. "I'm the manager. I'm not a head coach. I'm the manager."

School was out.

34

TINKER
TO EVERS
TO CHANCE

They didn't like each other.

But Joe Tinker, Johnny Evers, and Frank Chance, the Cubs' infield combo immortalized in a poem, were able to turn double plays despite the hostility.

Tinker and Evers battled each other. One story said the feud began in 1905 with an argument over a taxi, which Evers supposedly took and left Tinker waiting by the curb. Evers blamed the friction on an incident in 1907 when Tinker threw a ball harder than necessary at the second baseman that bent back one of Evers' fingers.

"Tinker and myself hated each other," Evers said, "but we loved the Cubs. We wouldn't fight for each other, but we'd come close to killing people for our team. That was one of the answers to the Cubs' success."

The high-strung Evers was nicknamed the "Human Crab" because of the way he crouched to slide and scoop up ground balls. The moniker might have been because of his disposition. Evers was always barking about something and argued with teammates, opponents, and umpires. He was ejected as a player 58 times.

The unhappiness with Chance was a little more complicated.

Chance was studying to be a dentist when he was discovered playing summer league games in California. He joined the Chicago team in spring 1898 as a backup catcher and outfielder and was moved to first base.

Bottom line: Frank Chance wasn't the most congenial. Chance threw beer bottles at Brooklyn fans, charged Giants pitcher Joe McGinnity during a game, and was called "the greatest amateur brawler of all time" by boxing legends Jim Corbett and John L. Sullivan.

The Cubs, naturally, named him their manager in 1905.

In 1906, Chance led the National League in runs scored and stolen bases. He was fearless, once racing from second base to steal home and break a tie game against the Reds. As a manager, Chance might have been ogrelike, but he was effective. More than just fearless, he was dubbed the "Peerless Leader" by Chicago sportswriter Charles Dryden

Frank Chance, Joe Tinker, and Johnny Evers (left to right)—in a rare reunion— didn't get along poetically during their playing days but, Evers said, "We loved the Cubs." (Getty Images)

and in 1906 led the Cubs to 116 wins (still a record, now shared—in a longer season—by the 2001 Mariners) and their first World Series, which they lost to the "hitless wonder" White Sox.

Chance didn't want his players socializing with members on the opposing team. He made outfielder Solly Hofman delay his wedding until after the baseball season was over to preserve his strength.

Tinker was moved from third base to shortstop in 1902 when he joined the Chicago Orphans (the formal team name evolved into "Cubs" over the decade), and the transition wasn't smooth, as he led all National

League shortstops with 72 errors in his first season. However, he did improve, leading the league in fielding percentage four times.

In an article in *Baseball Magazine*, F.C. Lane called Tinker and Evers the "Siamese twins of baseball" because "they play the bag as if they were one man, not two."

But in 1905 the friction—whatever the cause—carried over to the field, when the two came to blows before an exhibition game. (The enmity lingered, and they didn't speak to each other for more than 25 years.)

When Cubs owner Charles Murphy named Evers to replace Chance as player-manager in 1912, Tinker asked to be traded rather than play for someone he wasn't talking to. The Cubs shipped him to Cincinnati in an eight-player deal.

The three infielders first appeared in a game together on September 1, 1902, and turned their first double play two days later. Pitching and defense were key to the Cubs' success in the Deadball Era, and in 1906, they had a rotation that featured Mordecai Brown, Jake Pfiester, and Ed Reulbach backed by Tinker, Evers, and Chance.

Franklin Pierce Adams, a writer for the *New York Evening Mail*, had watched a Cubs–New York Giants game on July 11, 1910, and noted a key moment came in the eighth inning, when the Cubs' trio turned a double play.

It was listed in the box score as "Tinker to Evers to Chance." Adams was inspired. In those days, writers often added poetry at the end of their stories. Adams tacked on two lines to his column, "All in Good Humor":

"These are the saddest of possible words:
'Tinker to Evers to Chance.'"

Adams thought he was done for the day. But his column was six lines short for the paper, and he penned what is now known as "Baseball's Sad Lexicon":

These are the saddest of possible words:
"Tinker to Evers to Chance."
Trio of bear cubs, and fleeter than birds,
Tinker and Evers and Chance.
Ruthlessly pricking our gonfalon bubble,
Making a Giant hit into a double—

Words that are heavy with nothing but trouble:

"Tinker to Evers to Chance."

From 1906 to '10, the Cubs' trio combined for 491 double plays, third most in the National League at that time. The Cubs also won the NL pennant in 1906, '07, '08, and '10. The '08 team was, famously, the last Cubs team to win a World Series until 2016, when they ended a 108-year drought.

In August 2019, the Rosemont Convention Center, outside Chicago near O'Hare International Airport, was host to the National Sports Collectors Convention, a show crammed with tables stacked with boxes and display cases of photos and trinkets of all shapes and sizes. In the middle of the organized mess in the cavernous convention hall, three baseball jerseys hung in sparkling glass display cases.

There were no names or numbers on the back, but there was no mistaking which team they belonged to.

Tinker, Evers, and Chance certifiably once wore those jerseys. The garments were all wool, which had to be brutal on a hot August day at the ballpark, and were decorated sparsely. Two of the jerseys were from 1909 and featured CHICAGO down the front and the team nickname over the left chest. The other top was a Cubs home jersey from 1910 and had a standing bear holding a bat.

Their value? The jerseys, owned by a private collector, weren't for sale.

They were—like Mr. Adams' poem and the combination he immortalized—priceless.

35

LEE ELIA'S RANT

We all say things we regret. Lee Elia knows that too well.

The 1983 Cubs were 5–13 when the Dodgers came to Wrigley Field on April 29. The Cubs opened a 2–0 lead in the first inning, but the loaded Dodgers—who would finish the season atop the NL West—rallied and eventually won when Ken Landreaux scored the go-ahead run on a wild pitch by Lee Smith in the eighth.

At that time, the Cubs' clubhouse was located in the left field corner at Wrigley. As the players were exiting up the line, Keith Moreland and Larry Bowa got into separate arguments with some of the remaining 9,391 fans. Moreland was upset by their taunts; Bowa, always fiery anyway, was hit by a projectile, which got him more riled up.

So emotions were high when Elia delivered a postgame rant to the media—recorded, of course—that has lived on in transcripts, in replays (with and without bleeps), and in infamy. His tirade ripped the fans, highlighted by this: "Eighty-five percent of the fuckin' world is working. The other 15 come out here."

He also suggested what the fans could do and where they could do it, with an invitation to the assembled media: "And print it!"

The print media (editing only where necessary) printed it.

Elia was on Dallas Green's coaching staff when Green managed in Philadelphia. When Green took over as the Cubs' general manager, he hired Elia in 1982 to manage the team. On that fateful April day in '83, Green called his manager in the evening and said Elia had been a little "aggressive" during his media session.

"When I heard that tape, it [Elia's job] was in jeopardy, I'll guarantee that," Green told the *Chicago Tribune* the next day.

"I did say some things I really feel bad about," Elia told me several years later. "It kind of hurt me, because I love players and I didn't think there was any place better in the world to be than Chicago. You'd be a damn fool not to think they're the greatest fans in the world. They've suffered through defeats and still love the players.

"But when I made my comments about the fans, I honest to God was directing them at those people who went after Moreland and Bowa," Elia said. "I didn't mean the Chicago people in general. That was something I often hoped they would always understand, but that was unfortunate."

Elia apologized that night on Jack Brickhouse's radio show. He wasn't fired immediately; that came in August after another verbal misstep. The Cubs had lost 5–3 to the Braves and rookie first baseman Gerald Perry, who hit a solo homer and drove in three runs. After the game, Elia told reporters, "We've never heard of this guy Gerald Perry."

Well, Green had the scouting report on Perry and the Braves on his desk. Yes, they'd heard of the guy—and thought Elia's comment was a copout.

"That was an embarrassment to the team and the whole organization," Green told reporters. "Lee should have known better."

Bowa speculated that Elia had lost something since the April incident.

"He was tough early, but maybe the tirade against the fans changed things," Bowa told reporters that August. "He wasn't chewing people out or fining people. He wasn't the same man at the end that I knew."

Elia did manage again, taking over the Phillies in 1987 and continuing through 1988. Through it all and since, he's had to deal with his regrettable rant.

"There are so many beautiful and special things about Chicago," Elia, whose brief playing career included stops with both the White Sox and Cubs, told me. "I'm going to be the guy who probably feels the strongest about the history of Chicago and the beauty of the town, and I'll never be equated that way. I'll always be the guy who said something about the Chicago fans, and that's something I'll have to live with."

On the 25th anniversary of the tirade, Elia combined with a collectibles company to sell autographed baseballs packaged in a case that played a variation of the 1983 speech—but with a new, no-bleep-required message to Cubs fans:

"I'll tell you one thing. It's time the Cubs get hotter than hell this season and stuff it up the rest of the baseball world. The 40,000 fans who fill this ballpark every day and work hard for a living are no nickel-and-dimers. They deserve a championship. They're the real Chicago Cubs fans.

"And print it!"

36

2018
AND DAVID BOTE

In the second half of the 2016 season, David Bote was playing at Class A Myrtle Beach and pressing. He wasn't in the lineup every day and watched others get promoted. Bote wasn't a top prospect but was the Cubs' 18th-round pick in 2012 out of Neosho County Community College in Chanute, Kansas.

Would he ever make it to the big leagues? Bote had a young family to support.

"I said, 'Man, am I ever going to get a chance?'" Bote told me about a conversation he had with Cubs minor league manager Mark Johnson. "He said, 'You are. You have a jersey on your back.' I was like, 'You're right.' There were times I wanted to put the blame on somebody else, and he put it right back on me. He said, 'You have to take responsibility.'"

There were plenty of people who supported the young infielder, including his wife, Rachel.

"If I didn't have my wife, I'd probably be out of baseball," Bote said. "I was going back to high-A to play every day in 2016 and I was like, 'I'm done. I'm over it.' She was the one who said, 'Hey, we didn't stay in Class A ball for four years for you to give up now.'"

Bote didn't give up. And his determination—plus support from people like Rachel, Johnson, and others—propelled him not just to the big leagues but also to one of the most dramatic moments in the Cubs' 2018 season.

The Cubs were facing the Nationals on August 12 in the final game of a three-game series at Wrigley Field. It was a marquee matchup between Washington ace Max Scherzer and Cole Hamels, who was making his third start since the Cubs acquired the left-hander at the trade deadline.

The Cubs hoped Hamels would give the rotation a boost. After the euphoria of the Cubs' first World Series championship in 108 years in 2016, the '17 campaign had been a letdown, even though they reached the National League Championship Series for the third straight year.

The 2018 season was a chance for the Cubs to prove they were cured after the so-called hangover from '16. They had a 2½-game lead

CUBS AND WRIGLEY FIELD IN THE MOVIES

Did you snicker when you heard Elwood say his address was 1060 W. Addison in the movie *The Blues Brothers*? If you're a true Cubs fan, you knew that's Wrigley Field's home.

There is no shortage of great baseball movies, though the best seem to feature other teams (the Yankees, the Red Sox, the old Senators) and places (Iowa, Durham, Milwaukee imitating Cleveland). But Hollywood didn't altogether forget Wrigley Field and the Cubs. A sampling of favorites:

Elmer, the Great (1933)
Alibi Ike (1935)
Two ancient but fun movies starring comic actor Joe E. Brown as fictional Cubs, both films with creative links to famed scribe Ring Lardner. Ike's manager is played by William Frawley, Fred Mertz in *I Love Lucy*—here named "Cap," as in "Anson." Brown's son, Joe L., was general manager of the Pirates during their World Series seasons of 1960 and '71.

The Babe Ruth Story (1948)
Not the grim John Goodman biopic that came later; this one stars William Bendix as The Bambino and is absolutely ridiculous—and if you accept it as the corny fiction it is, it's pretty wonderful. Legendary Cub Charlie Root (who survived for 22 years after the movie's release) must have especially despised the 1932 "Called Shot" scene set in Wrigley Field. So did most serious critics. But you won't forget Johnny.

The Winning Team (1952)
The Pride of St. Louis (1952)
Big year for Hall-of-Fame pitcher bios. In *Winning*, Ronald Reagan stars as Grover Cleveland Alexander and Doris Day as his wife. Some Cubs moments here—Alec's bigger seasons were mostly elsewhere—but here's a chance to see the future pres in action off the gridiron. Dan Dailey, known mainly for his musicals, emulates Dizzy Dean well enough in *Pride*—and here, too, some Cubs moments, though Diz, great with the Cards, was running on fumes and guile as a Cub. Curiously, both films grossed $1.7 million that year at the box office.

The Blues Brothers (1980)
A pure Chicago movie except for a Joliet cameo and that country-bar scene.

>Jake: "How are you gonna get the band back together, Mr. Hot Rodder? Those cops have your name, your address."
>Elwood: "They don't have my address. I falsified my renewal. I put down 1060 West Addison."

Wrigley's famous marquee does make an appearance.

Brewster's Millions (1985)
Included in this list even though the connection is thin because star Richard Pryor gets to wear a Cubs uniform in this comedy and in just about every publicity photo ever published. The film also features John Candy as—what else?—a catcher.

Ferris Bueller's Day Off (1986)
Sneaky but endearing suburbanite Ferris (Matthew Broderick) leads his friends astray as they skip school and explore Chicago—including, of course, Wrigley Field, where he and his pals urge players to "suh-WING, battah." And, of course, he catches a foul ball. The scene was shot during a Braves–Cubs game on June 5, 1985, a 4–2 Cubs loss.

A League of Their Own (1992)
Baseball owners decide to create a league of women players to maintain revenue streams while lots of MLB stars are fighting World War II. Garry Marshall is Walter Harvey, standing in for Phil Wrigley, who really was part of this; Wrigley Field stars as "Harvey Field" during tryouts. Lots of almost-true stuff here, as the actual All-American Girls Professional Baseball League is treated affectionately. Apart from the ballpark, no more Cubs stuff—though tobacco-chewing Tom Hanks, as the Rockford Peaches manager, will remind some of somebody Cub-like. They'll be wrong.

Rookie of the Year (1993)
Henry Rowengartner (Thomas Ian Nicholas) plays a 12-year-old who breaks his arm and, after the cast is removed, realizes he can throw 100 mph. In the last game of the season, the Cubs need a win against the Mets. But he injures his arm and...no spoiler here. Directed by Daniel Stern, who in real life is smarter than the idiot he played in two *Home Alone* films.

in the Central Division when Hamels faced the Nationals on that perfect summer night in Chicago. Washington took a 1–0 lead in the second inning and made it 3–0 in the ninth after a two-run single by Ryan Zimmerman off Brandon Kintzler.

Bote was watching the game unfold from the bench. In the Cubs' ninth, Nats reliever Ryan Madson retired the first batter, then gave up a single to Jason Heyward, hit Albert Almora Jr. with a pitch, and, one out later, plunked Willson Contreras with a pitch to load the bases.

Manager Joe Maddon signaled for Bote to bat for pitcher Justin Wilson.

Bote knew Madson could throw a sinker and a four-seam fastball. The count was 2–2, and Bote told himself to just "hit it as hard as I can to center field." And that's what he did.

Bote sent the crowd of 36,490 into a frenzy with a game-winning, walk-off grand slam, launching the ball to straightaway center and powering the Cubs to a 4–3 victory.

Plenty of players fantasize about hitting such a home run. Bote actually did it.

"This is the ultimate excitement," Hamels said. "It's the thing that when you're a kid in the backyard and you're visualizing trying to win games, it's always bases loaded, you're down by three, and trying to hit the grand slam, and for Bote to be able to do it, what a way to be able to experience that."

Bote recalled hitting just two other grand slams ever, one in high school and another in the minors.

"He's the kind of guy who gets overlooked," Maddon said of the late-round pick. "He's not talked about often until he does something spectacular. He's one of those guys who has to show it for people to believe it."

Bote had come a long way—literally. He found out the Cubs drafted him when he was marooned at an airport in Mombasa, Kenya. At the time, he was on a mission trip with Rachel, who was then his girlfriend, and his older brother, Danny. Their plane had been diverted. Danny had somehow gotten an internet connection and discovered David had been drafted by the Cubs.

"There was no call or 'We're going to draft you,' or 'We're looking to draft you in this round,'" Bote told me. "It was in the airport—it's 'Hey, the Cubs drafted you in the 18th round.' I'm like, 'Hey, let's get out of here.'"

They did eventually reach their destination in Nairobi and fulfilled their mission obligation to set up a sports camp for children, who were used to playing soccer with a ball made of trash bags wrapped tight with string. Going 0-for-4 is nothing compared to what those kids had to deal with.

"In our view, they have nothing, but they have everything, in their eyes," Bote said. "They appreciate what they have and appreciate the love and their family. And the whole community they have that supports each other is something you don't see very much. It's eye-opening."

So was Bote's performance on that August night. The pinch-hit grand slam capped one of 48 come-from-behind wins that season by the Cubs, the most in the majors. The list included an amazing nine-run rally in the eighth inning on April 14 against the Braves, when the Cubs overcame a 10–2 deficit to win 14–10.

However, the Brewers were also surging that September. After 162 games, the Cubs and Brewers were tied at 95–67 and needed to play Game 163 to determine who would be the Central Division winner and who would play the Rockies as a wild-card entry.

This time, there was no magical comeback. The Brewers won 3–1 at Wrigley Field. And the Cubs' postseason lasted one game as they were ousted by the Rockies in the wild-card game 2–1 in 13 innings.

The Brewers and Rockies celebrated at Wrigley on back-to-back nights. The Cubs could only watch.

And in that wild-card game, David Bote—the hero of August 12, the 18th-round pick who on that night did something spectacular—batted twice and struck out twice.

But he would never be overlooked again. Believe it.

37

MAY 17, 1979

"**N**obody will ever know without many hours with the box score and a record book just how many records of ancient and modern major league baseball were smashed at the north side park yesterday. Cubs and Phillies hooked up in what was advertised as a baseball game but early proved to be a comic opera arranged to the tune of base hits."

That was the lede of *Chicago Tribune* sportswriter Frank Schreiber's game story on August 26, 1922—although it could have easily been used about a Cubs–Phillies game on April 17, 1976. Or about another Cubs–Phillies game, on May 17, 1979.

These two teams played some wacky games.

Let's start with the 1922 contest, and introduce you to left fielder Hack Miller, the son of a circus strongman. Miller hit two home runs and drove in six in the Cubs' 26–23 victory over the Phillies at Cubs Park on that August day. Schreiber wrote: "The first inning was the only one that resembled a ball game." Chicago manager Bill Killefer's team trailed 3–1 and then sent 13 batters to the plate in the second inning to score 10 runs. The Cubs added 14 more runs in the fourth.

Miller was something of a local legend. He was so strong, he would hammer nails through boards using his hand. He apparently had a tough time maintaining proper playing weight, and his big-league baseball career lasted just six seasons.

The Cubs and Phillies set a major league record for total runs scored by two teams (51) and total hits (51) in that '22 game. They were just getting warmed up.

In the 1976 game, the Cubs—evidently encouraged by a friendly southerly wind at Wrigley Field—opened a 12–1 lead after three innings. Lefty Steve Carlton, the Phillies' starter, lasted just 1⅔ innings, giving up seven runs on seven hits and two walks. In the Cubs' second, Steve Swisher hit a solo home run, Rick Monday followed with a three-run homer, Bill Madlock added an RBI double, and Manny Trillo hit an RBI single to chase Carlton.

But the Phillies had Mike Schmidt, who belted four home runs. He smacked a two-run shot in the fifth and a bases-empty homer in the seventh off Rick Reuschel, plus a three-run homer against Mike Garman in the eighth and a game-winning two-run blast in the 10th off Paul Reuschel. The Phillies won 18–16 in 10 innings.

"This was my best day in the majors," said Swisher, who had four RBIs. But it also was one of the most frustrating. Swisher was the Cubs' catcher, and Schmidt was hitting every kind of pitch that he called.

"I needed a boost like this," Schmidt told the *Chicago Tribune*'s Richard Dozer. "It just happened to come in a monstrous fashion."

Three years later, the Phillies' third baseman delivered again, hitting two home runs in a wild 23–22 win over the Cubs. Yes, the wind was blowing out at Wrigley Field.

"We all knew it was going to be one of those kinds of days," the Phillies' Larry Bowa said. "I mean, what the heck, the Cubs had a field-goal kicker warming up on the sidelines for three innings."

Or as Cubs broadcaster Jack Brickhouse said during the game: "This is not exactly a connoisseur's delight."

But it was unforgettable. The two teams combined for 50 hits, including 11 home runs. Bill Buckner hit a grand slam and finished with seven RBIs for the Cubs, and Dave Kingman hit three home runs, including one that hit a front porch on Kenmore Avenue beyond the left field bleachers. Neither starting pitcher (Randy Lerch for the Phils, Dennis Lamp for the Cubs) finished the first inning.

The Cubs—who had trailed 17–6 in the fourth—scored three runs in the eighth to tie the game at 22. There were two outs in the 10th when Schmidt came to bat for the eighth time and worked the count to 3–2 against the Cubs' Bruce Sutter. The Phillies slugger then launched a hanging split-finger fastball over the bleachers in left for the game-winner.

"I thought I had run the gamut of emotion in that 18–16 game against the Cubs a couple of years ago," Schmidt said afterward, "but this one tops anything I've ever seen. It can only happen in this park."

Schmidt would finish his 18-year career with more home runs at Wrigley Field (50) than any other road ballpark and more against the Cubs (78) than any other team.

And he and Sutter would, of course, both be inducted into the Hall of Fame. Neither of their plaques would mention that wild, windy May afternoon in Chicago.

38

TOM RICKETTS AND THEO EPSTEIN

Tom Ricketts and his siblings were just like other Cubs fans. They wanted the team to win a World Series.

Tom; brothers, Pete and Todd; and sister, Laura, however, did what most fans can only dream of. The Rickettses were able to purchase the Cubs in October 2009, for $845 million. At their introductory question-and-answer session at the Cubs Convention in January 2010, they made it clear this was not an impulse purchase.

"We're here for the long run," Tom Ricketts said. "We've made a commitment for this to be an intergenerational thing. We're looking at a 95-year timeline."

The Rickettses said they had three goals: they wanted to improve Wrigley Field and the surrounding area; they wanted to be good neighbors in the community; and they wanted the Cubs to win a World Series.

The last item on their wish list would require some patience and some help from Theo Epstein.

The Rickettses weren't Chicagoans. They grew up in Omaha, Nebraska, and adopted the Cubs as most of the team's out-of-town fans did—by watching WGN-TV on cable. Tom followed his older brother, Pete, to attend the University of Chicago and became a diehard fan in 1984 when the Cubs won the National League East. The two lived in an apartment at the corner of Addison and Sheffield, across the street from Wrigley Field.

They spent their summers in the bleachers, where Tom met his wife, Cecelia. Pete and Tom were soon joined in Chicago by Laura, who spent a summer with her brothers in Wrigleyville. Younger brother Todd eventually moved there as well.

"Being immersed in Wrigleyville on game day with the sights and the smells and the fans and the energy, and just the whole feel—the Cubs are bigger than us as owners," Laura said. "They're bigger than Wrigley itself. They're an emerging character. I think that being immersed in that, I had no choice but to become a Cubs fan. It was really overwhelming."

The Cubs hit the market in 2007. The *Chicago Tribune* had purchased the team in 1981 from the Wrigley family, who had owned the ballclub since 1919. Businessman Sam Zell announced his intention to acquire Tribune in April 2007 but said he would sell the Cubs. That sparked Tom Ricketts' pursuit of the team and the ballpark.

The complicated purchase took nearly three years to complete. When it was finalized, the Cubs had a family in charge rather than a corporation, which made a huge difference to the players and the fans. Now their owner had a face.

"You have a personal attachment now, somebody you can shake hands with and say, 'That's my boss,'" former Cubs pitcher Ryan Dempster said.

Plus, Cubs fans had someone in charge who knew what it was like to watch a game from the bleachers at Wrigley Field.

"The great part about this family and what's different from all the groups [who bid for the Cubs] is their agenda is, 'We're fans, we're legitimate fans, and we understand what the fan experience is like,'" said Crane Kenney, Cubs president of business operations and a Tribune Company holdover. "Which means they know what the restrooms look like, they know what concession lines look like, they know how hard it is to park around here and they want to improve on all those things."

But Tom Ricketts also knew the Cubs needed to improve the baseball side of the business—and in October 2011, he hired Epstein to be the architect.

Epstein had gained credibility as a young general manager with the Red Sox, leading that team to the World Series in 2004, which ended an 86-year championship drought. Boston won again under Epstein in 2007. The Cubs, meanwhile, were riding the longest professional championship dry spell, having last won a World Series in 1908.

"I was ready for the next big challenge," Epstein said at his introductory news conference.

He stressed the importance of "building a foundation of sustained success" and created a textbook titled *The Cubs Way*. A Yale graduate, Epstein—born in New York but raised just outside Boston—grew up with an appreciation of the game as well as of ballparks like Fenway Park and Wrigley Field.

EDDIE VEDDER

Imagine having Ernie Banks, one of your childhood heroes, ask you to write a song about the Cubs, your favorite baseball team. No pressure, right? Eddie Vedder, who first went to games at Wrigley Field when he was growing up in Evanston, Illinois, accepted the challenge.

Vedder, now the lead vocalist for the band Pearl Jam, was attending Randy Hundley's fantasy camp in Arizona when Banks made the request. So Vedder went back to his hotel room, scribbled some lyrics down, and created "All the Way," released in 2008, which also happened to be the 100th anniversary—if you can call it that—since the Cubs last won a World Series.

Banks was dazzled and told Vedder that the song captured "what I think about when I wake up in the morning."

Pearl Jam first performed the song on August 2, 2007, at the Vic Theatre, four blocks from Wrigley Field. During one of the band's concerts at Wrigley Field, Banks joined Vedder on stage to sing along.

Here's part of the song:

"We are one with the Cubs,
With the Cubs we're in love.
Hold our heads high as the underdogs.
We are not fair-weather, but foul-weather fans.
Like brothers in arms, in the streets and the stands.
There's magic in the ivy and the old scoreboard.
The same one I stared at as a kid keeping score.
In a world full of greed, I could never want more.
And someday we'll go all the way."

Vedder used to sit in the bleachers, and he worshipped Cubs outfielder Jose Cardenal. The outfielder would sign autographs for youngsters after games outside of Wrigley, which is how they met. Of course, at that time, Vedder was 12 or 13 years old and not a famous rock musician.

They formally met in 2002 when Cardenal was a coach on the Reds. Since then, Cardenal has been invited to Pearl Jam concerts and sat with Vedder during Cubs playoff games. In 2004, Vedder's wife surprised him by inviting the outfielder to his birthday party.

"It's a great relationship," Cardenal told me. "I've known him since he was a kid. You never know."

"To me," Epstein said, "baseball is better with tradition, baseball is better with history, baseball is better with fans who care, baseball is better with ballparks like this, baseball is better during the day, and baseball is best of all when you win."

That, ultimately, was why Ricketts wanted Epstein.

Epstein reunited key personnel who had helped him in Boston, hiring general manager Jed Hoyer and minor league and scouting director Jason McLeod. With the band back together, one of their first projects was to strengthen the Cubs' minor league talent pool so the team didn't have to rely on expensive free agents.

However, when Epstein took over the Red Sox, he inherited a team that was coming off a 93-win season and a second-place finish in the American League East. When he joined the Cubs, this team didn't have a set first baseman, third baseman, or right fielder; the pitching was suspect; and the defense was the worst in the National League. The Cubs had finished fifth in the then six-team NL Central in 2010 and '11, would stay there in Epstein's first season, then—during Epstein's rebuild—finish last in the now five-team division for two more seasons. And yet...

"Within a few minutes of talking to him, I had a good feeling that this was the right guy for us," Tom Ricketts said of Epstein. "When he came in, he's very low-key, very thoughtful, very team oriented—all the things I thought would be great not only for the baseball side but for building a great baseball culture. It just all kind of fit."

Epstein's first deal was essentially for himself. Because he had one year remaining on his contract with the Red Sox, Major League Baseball determined that Boston was entitled to compensation. The Cubs eventually sent reliever Chris Carpenter to the Red Sox, and the two teams later exchanged two more players, with reliever Aaron Kurcz going to Boston in exchange for Jair Bogaerts, Xander's twin brother, a young catcher–first baseman.

"If you're going to pick two teams to play for, why not have it be the Cubs and the Red Sox? You can't complain about that," said Carpenter, who will forever be the answer to the trivia question: Who was traded for Theo Epstein?

The right-hander appeared in just eight games for the Red Sox in 2012 and pitched one season in Japan in 2014. Jair Bogaerts would never play in the big leagues; Kurcz, who bounced around in the minors for a decade, was last seen in 2019 pitching for Tijuana in the Mexican League.

"Theo mania" took over Wrigleyville. Soon after he was hired, THEOLOGY T-shirts were for sale.

Not every move by Epstein and Co. worked. In December 2011, Epstein dealt infielder DJ LeMahieu and outfielder Tyler Colvin to the Rockies for third baseman Ian Stewart and a pitcher. Stewart batted .201 in an injury-filled season in 2012, then complained about playing time. He was released in June 2013. LeMahieu, the Cubs' second-round pick in 2009, evolved into an All-Star, Gold Glove winner, and two-time batting champion.

In July 2013, Epstein did orchestrate one of the best deals in Cubs history when he sent pitcher Scott Feldman and catcher Steve Clevinger to the Orioles for pitchers Jake Arrieta and Pedro Strop. And Epstein won the bidding war for free agent Jon Lester in December 2014, reuniting with the left-hander who had pitched for the Red Sox from 2006 to '14. Arrieta, Strop, and Lester would play key roles for the Cubs in 2016.

Ricketts trusted Epstein when the Cubs acquired controversial closer Aroldis Chapman for highly touted prospect Gleyber Torres and three other players in July 2016. Chapman had begun that season under a 30-game suspension because of a domestic abuse allegation that did not result in charges. The Cubs desperately needed a closer to maximize their chances in the postseason, especially one who could throw 100-mph fastballs.

"If not now, when?" Epstein said of the rationale for the move.

Epstein was upfront regarding the Cubs' rebuilding plans, telling fans they needed to be patient. The addition of manager Joe Maddon in 2015 accelerated the team's progress. The Cubs reached the postseason that year as a wild-card team, then ended their 108-year championship drought the next year by winning the World Series.

Epstein's first three first-round draft picks—Albert Almora Jr., Kris Bryant, and Kyle Schwarber—were all on the 2016 team and contributed in Game 7.

Epstein had planned on staying with the Cubs for at least 10 years, but on November 17, 2020, he made the surprising announcement that he was stepping down.

Doing so at that time was designed to hopefully ease the transition to Jed Hoyer, who was promoted from general manager. Epstein, who had one year left on his contract, said there were decisions that had to be made regarding the Cubs' long-term future, especially as the team dealt with financial uncertainty related to COVID-19. Hoyer is "more than ready to lead the Cubs into their next chapter," Epstein said at his farewell news conference.

Although he didn't announce any immediate plans, Epstein did sound like a Cubs fan when talking about his future. He couldn't wait to bring his family to a game at Wrigley Field.

"It will feel like home," he said.

What he didn't anticipate was the response from fans after the 2016 season.

"Virtually every day someone will come up to me, strangers, and share what the World Series meant to them and to their family and start sharing intimate details of relationships in their family, growing up watching the Cubs together," Epstein said. "That is such a privilege. Where else in life can you get that?"

Tom Ricketts knows that feeling. While Epstein's focus was on the team, the Ricketts family pursued their other goals. In 2014, they began a $1 billion renovation project of Wrigley Field, which included creating a park along the west side of the ballpark to be used year-round. The quirky immediate neighborhood where the Rickettses once rented an apartment has since evolved to include a hotel, new restaurants, and a large office building.

Tom Ricketts could often be spotted in the upper deck or on the concourse at Wrigley Field during games, mingling with the customers. He would stop to shake hands, pose for selfies, hear folks say "thank you," and also listen to a complaint or two.

Fans quickly discovered that he's just a regular guy—who happens to be worth millions—who's responsible for a team bigger than him and his family, and bigger than Wrigley itself.

39

MORDECAI "THREE-FINGER" BROWN

Mordecai "Three Finger" Brown pitched in four World Series for the Cubs, has one of the most accurate nicknames in all of sports, and still holds franchise pitching records that most likely will never be broken.

But one of the things Brown liked most was to help others, and he has continued to do that more than 70 years after his death.

Brown was a third baseman for a semi-pro team in 1898 and was asked to pitch when the pitcher didn't show up for a game. His pitches had quite a bit of movement because of his unique grip.

There are a few stories about how Brown lost two fingers on his right hand, stories embellished by the media in the 1900s. Some said one of his brothers dared him to put his hand in a piece of farm machinery and it chopped them off.

"Mordecai's own account was that when he was five years old, he was on his uncle's farm," Scott Brown, a distant relative, told me. "His uncle was chopping silage—cutting corn stalks and things to feed the cows—and he was using a corn chopper, which is kind of like a trough and had these moving blades in the middle of it.

"Here's a five-year-old boy, inquisitive—whether it was an accident, whether it was curiosity, whether he was helping put the cornstalks through, regardless—he put his hand under the moving blade, and it took off his index finger."

At the time, the Browns lived in Nyesville, Indiana, in the west-central part of the state, and the doctor there was a veteran of the Civil War. He bandaged Brown's hand "battle style," wrapping the index finger to the middle finger to keep it steady. However, a few days later, Brown and his sister were chasing a pet rabbit around the farm and he slipped and jammed his right hand against the bottom of a washtub. The youngster didn't want to tell anyone and left it alone.

When the doctor unwrapped Brown's right hand, the middle finger was crooked because it was broken by the fall and healing incorrectly. The boy was left with an index finger that was chopped off and a middle finger that was twisted and mangled and growing back wrong. His third finger had some nerve damage as well, and he didn't have a lot of feeling in it. So, the only two digits on his hand that Brown had full functionality with were his pinky and his thumb.

"And that's what he used to throw the devastating curveball that Ty Cobb said was impossible to hit," Scott Brown said.

After two spectacular seasons in the minors, Brown made his major league debut with the St. Louis Cardinals in 1903. That December, after he went 9–13 with the Cards, they dealt him to the Cubs—and he thrived.

The right-hander pitched for the Cubs from 1904 to 1912 and led them to two World Series championships (1907 and '08). In 1906, he went 26–6 with a 1.04 ERA in 36 games and completed 27 of his 32 starts. He won 29 games in 1908, and in '09 led the league with 27 wins, 50 games, and 32 complete games.

Brown still holds the Cubs' team pitching records for most wins in a single season (29) and is the franchise leader in career complete games (206), shutouts (48), and ERA (1.80).

He worked on his accuracy by aiming rocks at knotholes on the wall of a smokehouse. Scott Brown said they actually had Mordecai's grip analyzed by professionals, including Cubs pitcher Fergie Jenkins.

Did his mangled hand help Brown or hurt him? We'll never really know.

"There were those who told us, yeah, the delivery became a weird, twisted circle-change, and yes, it did give him a little bit of an oddity in his delivery," Scott Brown said, "but the reality was he was kind of a freak of nature and a phenom."

Catcher Jimmy Archer, who starting in 1909 was Mordecai Brown's teammate on the Cubs, recalled warming him up for a game at the West Side Grounds, their pre-1914 home. Umpire Bill Klem was watching and went up to the catcher and bumped him off the plate. Klem dropped a piece of paper the size of a silver dollar behind the plate.

"He said, 'Brown doesn't need you—that's the only target he needs,'" Scott Brown said, relaying the story. "Archer said he was absolutely correct."

One of Brown's best games was one he didn't start. On October 8, 1908, the Cubs were playing the New York Giants to determine which team would win the NL pennant. The great Christy Mathewson started

1906 CUBS WORLD SERIES

For six days in October, Chicago was the baseball center of the earth. It was 1906, and the Cubs, who had won a record 116 games and boasted the game's best offense, pitching, and defense, were facing the "hitless wonder" White Sox in the World Series.

"Last night, Chicago was baseball mad," the *Chicago Tribune*'s Hugh Fullerton wrote on October 4, 1906, the day after the White Sox had clinched the American League pennant to set up the first World Series to be played in one city. "Crowds stood cheering on corners at the mention of the game, everywhere there was rejoicing. Men stood and cheered in elevated trains when the news was passed along that the Sox were safe and that Chicago had two pennants—and the world's championship."

They were two different teams. The Cubs had surged to a 29–15 record after April and May and clinched the National League pennant on September 19 with more than two weeks remaining in the season. The White Sox, led by manager Fielder Jones, did not have a single regular hit over .300.

The intracity World Series was played over six consecutive days, beginning October 9, and alternated at each team's home ballpark. It also was a chance for the city to celebrate, as the series began nearly 35 years to the day after the Great Chicago Fire, which had left more than 100,000 residents homeless.

Game 1 was at the Cubs' West Side Grounds, and City Hall workers were given the day off to attend. But a lot of working-class baseball fans didn't have that luxury, because they had to be at their jobs. White Sox owner Charles Comiskey was a little upset because he wanted rowdy Sox fans in the stands. Major League Baseball also forced the two teams to double their ticket prices, so the most expensive ticket was $2 (remember, it's 1906; Sears was selling men's suits in that year's catalog for $4.45).

Fans lined up hours before the first pitch to try and purchase a 50-cent bleacher ticket. The *Chicago Tribune* created watch-party sites downtown at the First Regiment Armory and the McVicker's Theater, where someone would announce the game action through a megaphone, relying on ticker-tape updates.

The Cubs were the heavy favorites and started 26-game winner Mordecai "Three Finger" Brown in Game 1. But he was outpitched by Nick Altrock as the White Sox won 2–1. The Cubs tied the best-of-seven series with a 7–1 win in Game 2 at South Side Park behind Ed Reulbach's one-hitter.

There was no home-field advantage, as the White Sox won Game 3 3–0 at West Side Grounds when Ed Walsh threw a two-hitter. Brown answered with a two-hit shutout in Game 4 to even the series at two wins apiece.

Cubs manager Frank Chance, who had about a dozen nicknames, including P.L. for "Peerless Leader," tried to change his team's luck by having them wear their road uniforms at home in Game 5. Bear cubs were paraded at the park. The White Sox committed six errors but still won 8–6.

The World Series was the talk of the town, although the *Chicago Tribune* did run a story on October 14 about a butcher named Ulrich Schulte who the newspaper claimed was the only man in Chicago who didn't know about baseball's championship. Police had their hands full. One man, Cubs fan John J. Ryan, apparently attacked a crowd of White Sox supporters by himself.

Chance tabbed Brown to pitch on one day's rest in Game 6, but the Cubs ace gave up seven runs on eight hits over 1⅔ innings and took the loss 8–3 in front of 19,249 at South Side Park. White Sox pitchers combined for a 1.33 ERA in the six games.

"The White Sox played better ball and deserved to win," Cubs owner Charles Murphy said to fans. "I am for Chicago and will say that Chicago has the two best ball teams in the world."

White Sox fans had bragging rights and paraded through the city in celebration. Despite the loss, Chance still boasted about his team.

"It was the greatest series ever played, and we have got to give it to Comiskey's champions," Chance told reporters. "The Sox played grand, game baseball and outclassed us in this series just ended.

"But there is one thing I never will believe, and that is that the White Sox are a better ball club than the Cubs. We did not play our game, and that's all there is to it. The Sox, on the contrary, were fighting us in the gamest kind of a way. They fought so hard that they made us like it and like it well. We played our hardest to win, but in this series we did not show we were the best club."

That season was the first of a tremendous run by the Cubs—still the best five-year stretch by any team in baseball—in which they averaged 106 wins and would reach the World Series four times, winning in 1907 and '08 but losing to the Philadelphia Athletics in 1910.

Imagine if the Cubs and White Sox faced off in a World Series now: Men (and women) would stand at nighttime and cheer in elevated trains when the news was shared on smartphones...

for the Giants against the Cubs' Jack Pfiester. But Cubs manager Frank Chance pulled Pfiester after he gave up one run in the first inning, and Brown went 8⅓ innings in the 4–2 win.

"I was about as good that day as I ever was in my life," Brown said.

A writer from the *New York World* wrote: "The only thing for [Giants manager John] McGraw to do to beat Chicago is to dig up a pitcher with only two fingers."

Mathewson and Brown met 25 times, including the last big-league starts ever for both pitchers on September 4, 1916, in the second game of a Cubs–Cincinnati doubleheader in Weeghman Park. They'd agreed to pitch to help boost attendance in the Labor Day matchup. Both went nine innings, and the Reds won 10–8, with Mathewson getting the win. It wasn't a masterpiece: Brown gave up 19 hits, Mathewson 15.

In 14 seasons, Brown won 239 games. The pitcher died in 1948, but he is still helping the game through the Mordecai Brown Legacy Foundation, which great-nephew Fred Massey helped create. Mordecai did not have any children of his own, so it's been up to other family members. Scott Brown is a first cousin three times removed, which means Mordecai's grandfather and Scott's great-great-grandfather were the same person.

The original impetus for the foundation was to keep Mordecai's legacy, image, and history alive, Scott Brown said. Besides protecting the name, the foundation also works with college summer leagues to provide equipment and some life-coaching materials.

A three-foot-high granite monument honoring Mordecai Brown is on some farmland in Nyesville.

Scott Brown heard from a family who were driving through Parke County, Indiana, while on vacation. A preteen daughter was in the backseat and she wasn't happy because the car radio couldn't pick up the Cubs' broadcast that day.

"They're driving through the county and heading to see a historic place called Billie Creek Village," Scott Brown said. "The daughter happens to look up and see a sign. As her mother put it, she screams from the backseat—'Daddy, stop the car, turn around. It says Mordecai Brown Memorial this way.'"

She knew her Cubs history.

Mordecai Brown's pitching hand was mangled after two farm accidents but it helped him throw a devastating curve that Ty Cobb said was impossible to hit.
(Everett Collection/Newscom)

"He was always looking to empower others with the idea that they could go past their limitations, that they could achieve excellence over adversity," Scott Brown said of his famous relative. "He spent a lifetime making certain that others understood what they could achieve."

No matter how many fingers.

40

KYLE SCHWARBER

Kyle Schwarber was recruited by Ohio State to play linebacker. Instead, he decided to focus on hitting home runs into the stratosphere at Indiana. He made an impression. Observed Cubs super scout Stan Zielinski: "He has the best college bat I've seen in a long time, and remember I'm old, so I've seen a lot of them."

So the Cubs took Schwarber in the first round (fourth overall) of the 2014 draft. The payoff came quickly: in Game 4 of the 2015 National League Division Series, Schwarber—officially still in his rookie year—launched an epic homer onto the top of the video scoreboard in right field at Wrigley Field.

But it was in 2016—a season that nearly ended tragically—that Schwarber really revealed his superpowers.

The Cubs were playing the Diamondbacks at Chase Field in the third game of the season. In the D-backs' half of the second inning, Schwarber, playing left field, and center fielder Dexter Fowler both ran full speed after Jean Segura's fly ball toward the gap in left center. As both reached for the ball, the two outfielders became tangled up and crashed to the ground. Segura didn't stop and was credited with an inside-the-park home run.

Fowler stayed in the game. Schwarber had to be carted off the field.

"It had bad things written all over it," Cubs manager Joe Maddon said. "The guy hits the ball in the one spot we can't cover."

"We both went at it, and I stuck my glove up and I was pretty close," Schwarber said. "We were playing hard. I have no regrets about playing hard and getting hurt."

It wasn't until the next day that Schwarber learned he had torn both the ACL and LCL in his left knee and sprained his left ankle in the collision. He was done for the season.

Schwarber admitted to feeling sorry for himself for about half an hour, then sent Cubs president of baseball operations Theo Epstein a text message saying he wanted the Cubs to win and to be with them during his rehab.

"That tells you all you need to know about a 23-year-old who is going through the first significant injury of his life and the only thing that matters to him right now is winning and staying a part of this team," Epstein said.

Epstein had learned firsthand about Schwarber's determination prior to the 2014 draft. The Cubs executive asked the Ohio native if he was serious about catching. Schwarber slammed his fist on the desktop, frustrated at being doubted. That conviction—and the quick, powerful bat—was all Epstein needed to see.

Even with Schwarber sidelined in 2016, the Cubs had a magical run, winning a major league–leading 103 games and the NL Central Division. While the team was finishing up the regular season in September, Schwarber had made enough progress to do agility drills in the outfield at Wrigley Field.

He went with the Cubs to San Francisco for the NL Division Series.

"It's reality—it is what it is," Schwarber said about being on the bench. "I'm embracing it and being able to yell as loud as I can to try to help them out."

He also continued to think like a catcher, watching video of the starting pitchers.

"I like to sit there and think, 'What's the possible options we can go with on this hitter?'" he said. "It's just a way to keep me in the game."

The Cubs beat the Giants in the NLDS to advance. Schwarber, again watching from the bench, was at Wrigley Field for Games 1 and 2 of the NL Championship Series against the Dodgers, then flew to Dallas on October 17 for his six-month checkup with Dr. Dan Cooper, the orthopedic surgeon who had repaired the knee.

And there, he got a surprise: the leg, Cooper told him, had healed enough so he could play, albeit in a limited way. Schwarber immediately called Epstein.

"With as hard as Kyle has worked and as much as this means to him and potentially to us, we wanted to give him the opportunity," Epstein said.

At that point, the Cubs and Dodgers were tied at one win apiece in the best-of-seven NLCS. If the Cubs reached the World Series, Schwarber could be the designated hitter in the American League ballpark. That was a big *if*, considering the Cubs had not made it to the championship since 1945.

Schwarber joined the Cubs in Los Angeles for Game 3, then went to the Cubs' complex in Mesa, Arizona, to take batting practice and hit 400 to 500 balls off a hitting machine. The only problem was the blisters on his hands from all the swings.

On October 22, he saw his first game action since the accident as the DH for the Mesa Solar Sox in an Arizona Fall League game. Between innings, he watched the Cubs' series-clinching win over the Dodgers in Game 6 on an iPad in the dugout.

His Solar Sox teammates sprayed him with champagne in the clubhouse so he could be part of the celebration in Chicago.

Schwarber played one more AFL game and then was added to the Cubs' World Series roster.

"I didn't anticipate it—did not anticipate it," Maddon said of Schwarber's unexpected return.

(Maybe Schwarber did. Before the surgery, Cooper had asked him to fill out a questionnaire with his goals. Schwarber wrote "World Series?"—including the question mark.)

It seemed fitting that Schwarber would make his return at Progressive Field in Cleveland, where he made his first big-league start in June 2015, going 4-for-5 with a triple and two RBIs.

On this night, Schwarber struck out in his first at-bat in Game 1 of the World Series against the Indians' Corey Kluber. But then he doubled with two outs in the fourth, becoming the first National League player (including pitchers) with a World Series hit and no regular season hits since Jesse Orosco did so in 1986. It wasn't enough, as the Cubs lost 6–0.

In Game 2, Schwarber hit an RBI single in the third inning and added another in the fifth as the Cubs evened the Series with a 5–1 victory behind Jake Arrieta.

"How about his at-bats? First hit of the year in the World Series—that's pretty impressive," David Ross said of his teammate.

Schwarber was still restricted in terms of what he could do in the field, so when the Series shifted to Wrigley Field and NL rules, Schwarber was back on the bench. Maddon told him to be ready for anything. Cubs fans saluted Schwarber during pregame introductions, which was much better than the home opener on April 11, when Schwarber had hobbled onto the field needing a crutch.

"I think our fans really appreciate how hard he worked to get back at this moment," Maddon said. "Not everyone would've done that."

Schwarber did get a pinch-hit at-bat in Game 3 but did not play in Games 4–5. The Indians had a 3–2 lead in the series when it returned to Cleveland. Schwarber would be back as the designated hitter.

"It gives them a little more balance," Indians manager Terry Francona said of Schwarber's presence. "We respect him, but we also respect the other guys, too. I'm sure they're excited about being able to play him and having his bat in the lineup."

Addison Russell provided the firepower in Game 6, hitting a grand slam and a two-run double to power the Cubs and force a deciding Game 7.

Schwarber—and Cubs fans—were feeling pretty good about their chances when Fowler led off Game 7 with a home run. Schwarber, moved up to second in the lineup, then singled and two outs later, forgot about his repaired left knee and stole second base. He didn't score, but the game was tied at 6 after nine innings. A brief rain delay created a perfect chance for the Cubs players to regroup.

Schwarber then delivered his biggest hit of the World Series when he led off the 10th with a single. He was lifted for pinch-runner Albert Almora Jr., who advanced on Kris Bryant's fly out and then scored the go-ahead run on Ben Zobrist's double. The Cubs added another run and held on for an 8–7 victory and their first World Series championship since 1908.

As for the home run ball on top of the video scoreboard: Schwarber would love to have it. Meanwhile, he'll settle for the championship ring—and an epic miracle.

41

1990 ALL-STAR GAME

Wrigley Field didn't need lights to host the 1947 and 1962 All-Star Games. But it took an intervention by National League president Bart Giamatti, a city council vote, and the installation of lights to get the event back to the ballpark in 1990.

A little history lesson:

From the first All-Star Game in 1933, played in Comiskey Park, through 1958, the game was an annual affair. With the exception of games in two war years (1943 in Philadelphia's Shibe Park and '44 at Forbes Field in Pittsburgh, both under the lights), all were played in daylight.

The "annual" part changed when Major League Baseball played two All-Star Games each year from 1959 to '62 to generate additional revenue for the players' pension fund. In 1962, one game was played on July 10 at Washington's D.C. Stadium, but never mind that now. A second was played on July 30 at Wrigley Field. Both were day games.

The Cubs' Ernie Banks, Billy Williams, and George Altman were among the NL reserves for the second game in '62, along with future Hall of Famers Hank Aaron, Stan Musial, and Frank Robinson. The Red Sox's Pete Runnels, the Angels' Leon Wagner, and the Tigers' Rocky Colavito each hit home runs to power the American League to a 9–4 win in front of 38,359 fans at Wrigley Field.

With Major League Baseball eager for additional exposure (and, ultimately, higher rights fees), the first nighttime All-Star Game in the modern era was played in 1968 at the Astrodome in Houston, and as hoped by MLB and NBC, television ratings soared. The game returned to daytime in 1969, and predictably ratings plummeted. The 1970 game, played at night in Cincinnati (and memorable for Pete Rose's crushing slide into Ray Fosse on a game-winning hit by the Cubs' Jim Hickman), was a ratings monster.

The lesson was learned: there would be no more afternoon All-Star Games. If Wrigley Field were to host the game again, it needed lights.

After Dallas Green became the Cubs' general manager following the 1981 season, he lobbied for lights, asserting the team was at a competitive disadvantage without them. But he found himself battling the Illinois General Assembly and the Chicago city council, which under pressure from community residents had both passed legislation that banned night games at Wrigley.

WAYNE MESSMER

He's sung at conventions, at hockey games, at fantasy camps, and in front of presidents. He's performed before a few hundred people and millions who have caught his singing prior to nationally televised sporting events. Wayne Messmer has been one of the prime voices at Wrigley Field since 1985, and does have a favorite Cubs moment or two, beginning with Game 5 of the 2016 World Series.

"That was unbelievable to be handed the mic," Messmer told me. "Okay, the world is watching, so sing 'God Bless America' and the national anthem. That's funny because people don't understand it's the exact same request that I would get if it were the River Grove Little League. What I have to do is exactly the same, there's just more people watching."

Messmer was the public address announcer for the Loyola University hockey team when a tape recording of the anthem broke before a game was to start. So, he took the microphone and sang it himself. And people heard him. The Chicago Blackhawks hired Messmer to sing the anthem, a duty he did for 13 seasons, even though the Chicago Stadium crowds' cheers would often drown out his voice.

He was hired as the Cubs' public address announcer in 1985 and would sing the anthem on the field, then hustle up the ramps at Wrigley Field to the press box, where he would introduce the players before each at-bat.

During the Cubs Convention, Messmer is often the host of an alumni session at the weekend fan fest, which has featured players such as Bobby Dernier, Gary Matthews, Lee Smith, and Rick Sutcliffe. Messmer has attended former catcher Randy Hundley's fantasy camp to sing the anthem for the final game and act as emcee for their awards banquet.

"Those guys love it—it means a lot to them," he said of the camp attendees.

CHICAGO CUBS

The Cubs pleaded their case. The Tribune Co., which owned the team at the time, noted that without changes, at least some playoff or World Series games would have to be moved under someone's lights to fulfill national postseason television obligations. In 1984, that actually became an issue: the Cubs won the NL East but, with no lights, lost home-field advantage in the five-game Championship Series; the Padres, despite

Messmer was a Milwaukee Braves fan growing up in southeast Wisconsin, and Eddie Mathews was his all-time favorite player. He had the chance to meet the third baseman during an old-timers game, spending a half hour chatting with Mathews in the dugout.

"It was just fun," Messmer said. "It was 'Please be the guy I want you to be,' and he was."

He's still singing despite a horrific incident in April 1994 when, while sitting in his car, he was shot in the neck. Messmer needed 10 hours of surgery to repair the damage caused by the bullet, which barely missed his vocal cords.

On April 28, 1995, before the Cubs' home opener, Messmer returned to sing the anthem.

Messmer will never forget September 27, 2001. Baseball had been shut down after 9/11. The Cubs' first home game after the layoff was at night against the Astros, and 38,154 were crammed into Wrigley Field.

"It was pretty darn emotional," Messmer said of singing before the game. "I strode out to the pitcher's mound that night and did 'America the Beautiful' and then the national anthem. That was pretty amazing, because that morning, Kathleen and I were picked up by a couple of guys with no sense of humor in a black unmarked car, Secret Service guys, to drive to O'Hare [Airport] to stand next to President [George W.] Bush at a private event and sing the anthem.

"The president says, 'It's time for us to start flying again,'" Messmer said. "Then a Spirit Airlines flight flew over and was taking off on his command. That was the same day. That was kind of cool.

"At the end of that night, when we sat down, I said, 'This was not your typical day.'"

Wrigley Field is not your typical workplace, either. Messmer appreciates the historic setting.

"I'm such a fan of history," he said. "You've got Babe Ruth, Gabby Hartnett, Jack Brickhouse—you could go on forever. Having been part of it has been fun for me."

a poorer season record, were awarded three night games in San Diego, won them all, and reached the World Series.

In February 1988, the Chicago city council again was debating whether to allow the Cubs to install lights. During the discussions, Giamatti phoned Chicago mayor Eugene Sawyer to say Wrigley Field had been selected as the site of the 1990 All-Star Game—but only if the council approved lights.

"The All-Star Game is a prize for whatever city gets it," Cubs chairman John Madigan told the *Chicago Tribune* later, "and I'm sure they [major league owners] would not have waited any longer."

Sawyer made his pitch, the vote was 29–19, and the Cubs were cleared to play eight night games in '88 and 18 in future seasons. (Over the years, that 18-game limit would seem quaint; as of 2020, the limit was up to 43, with the team seeking more.) The lights were installed just weeks after the vote, Wrigley's first night game was played that August—and, as promised, the Cubs would host the 61st edition of the All-Star Game on July 10, 1990, in Wrigley Field.

Before the game, eight All-Stars took part in a primitive version of today's "home run derby" (based loosely on a 1950s television competition). The competitors included Matt Williams, Bobby Bonilla, Darryl Strawberry, and the Cubs' own Ryne Sandberg, plus American League contenders Ken Griffey Jr., Jose Canseco, Mark McGwire, and Cecil Fielder.

Contestants were given two innings of five outs to hit as many homers as possible. Remarkable for July in Chicago, the wind was blowing in that evening. Result: a total of five were slugged in the event. Sandberg hit three of them—and won.

"I was just so pumped up, I wanted to do something special," Sandberg said afterward. "I could hear the fans."

(Earlier in the day, Andre Dawson celebrated his 36th birthday by signing a new contract that, at $3.2 million, made him the highest-paid Cub in history. "Any ballplayer in their right mind, players on the opposition who come to visit—not only Wrigley Field but the city of Chicago—fall in love with the city," Dawson told the *Tribune*. "I'm one of those players.")

The Giants' Will Clark and the Athletics' Canseco were the top All-Star vote-getters in their respective leagues. Banks threw out a ceremonial first pitch in front of a sellout crowd of 39,071. The Cubs were represented in the game by Sandberg, Dawson, and Shawon Dunston. They went a combined 0-for-7.

And in an echo of that first Wrigley game under the lights, rain started about an hour before the first pitch and eventually interrupted play in the seventh inning. But unlike 8-8-88, this game resumed—and ended in a 2–0 American League win, thanks to a two-run double in the seventh by Julio Franco off Rob Dibble. Franco's hit was the only extra-base hit in the game. The National League team managed only two hits—singles by Lenny Dykstra and Will Clark—a record low for the All-Star Game.

But the lights worked fine.

42

CHARLIE GRIMM

The manager of this team was a jovial guy who could play the banjo and would later be featured in a Norman Rockwell painting. Its star pitcher? It could've been a 22-game winner or it could've been a right-hander acquired in late July—it depends on who you ask. One of the top hitters grew up on a Wisconsin dairy farm and was denied a chance to serve his country during wartime because of chronic high blood pressure.

And, of course, there was the goat.

The 1945 Cubs were a colorful bunch led by manager Charlie Grimm, who had played for the team from 1925 to '36. In August 1932, the Cubs trailed the Pirates by five games, and Grimm was named to replace manager Rogers Hornsby. The team responded well and won the pennant that season.

"I had fun playing baseball," Grimm wrote in his autobiography. "I tried to make it fun for my players after I became manager. I was 'Jolly Cholly' and I always thought a pat on the back, an encouraging word, or a wisecrack paid off a lot more than a brilliantly executed work of strategy."

The St. Louis Cardinals had won the National League pennant three straight seasons, but the '45 Cubs got a boost in July when they acquired ace right-hander Hank Borowy from the Yankees for $97,500. He joined pitchers Hank Wyse, Claude Passeau, Paul Derringer, and Ray Prim. Borowy, who was 10–5 that half-year with the Yanks, would post an 11–2 record with the Cubs, who finished with 98 wins and headed to the World Series for the first time since 1938.

Who knew it would be another 71 years before the Cubs would reach the championship again?

The '45 Cubs had been unable to prep for the season at their Catalina Island, California, spring training site due to wartime travel restrictions, so they trained in French Lick, Indiana. Because of military obligations, not all the players were able to attend. When the Japanese did surrender on August 14, the Cubs celebrated with a 20–6 win over Brooklyn the next day, and they were on a roll.

They would finish the season leading the majors in batting, powered by Phil Cavarretta, who grew up near Wrigley Field and who paced the NL with a .355 batting average. Teammate Stan Hack, 35 and near the end of his career, batted .323. Andy Pafko, the dairy farmer, ranked among the league leaders with 110 RBIs. Cavarretta won the Most Valuable Player voting that year; Pafko finished fourth.

Their World Series opponent was the Detroit Tigers, whom the Tinker-Evers-Chance Cubs had beaten back in 1907 and '08 but had lost to, under Grimm, in 1935.

Grimm tabbed Borowy to start Game 1 in Detroit, and he threw a six-hit shutout in a 9–0 win. Wyse, who was 22–10 for the season, started Game 2 and gave up a three-run homer to Hank Greenberg and the Cubs lost 4–1, but Passeau got the Cubs back on track at Briggs Stadium in Game 3, giving up just Rudy York's second-inning single in a 3–0 Chicago victory. The series shifted to Wrigley Field, and the Tigers scored all the runs they needed in the fourth inning off Prim in a 4–1 win to square the series at two apiece.

Borowy started Game 5 but was roughed up, giving up five runs over five innings in an 8–4 loss. In Game 6, Grimm started Passeau, then followed with Wyse and Prim out of the bullpen. When they failed to hold a lead in the eighth, the manager called on Borowy again to start the ninth—and stayed with the right-hander as the game went to extra innings.

In the end, Borowy would hurl four innings of shutout relief and the Cubs would win 8–7 on Stan Hack's 12th-inning RBI double off Dizzy Trout. The series would be tied at three games apiece. The decision went to Borowy.

Grimm could've picked Wyse—who had pitched to six batters the day before and not well—to start Game 7 but instead tabbed Borowy yet again. And Borowy gave up three straight singles to open the game and was pulled. All three would score, the inning ended with the Tigers leading 5–0, and the Cubs would lose the game 9–3, and the World Series.

"We didn't lose that World Series," Wyse told me. "Charlie Grimm did. Because he pitched Borowy all the time. He pitched the one he thought would win. I can't imagine me winning 22 and [starting] one game in a seven-game series. Sure, I was disappointed. A lot of other players were disappointed, too."

And that brings us to the goat.

Billy Sianis, who owned a West Side Chicago tavern, had saved the animal after it fell off a truck and broke its leg. Because business improved after it arrived, Sianis thought the goat brought his restaurant good luck.

He decided to bring the goat to Game 4 at Wrigley Field, and made a blanket that said, "We got Detroit's goat." The Andy Frain ushers tried to keep the animal out, but Sianis told them to check with team owner Philip Wrigley. The problem, it seemed, was that the goat smelled, so Sianis and his pet left.

Chicago reporters used to hang out at Sianis' tavern, and according to Rick Kogan's book, *A Chicago Tavern: A Goat, a Curse, and the American Dream*, Sianis told them about being ejected. After the Cubs lost the World Series, he sent a telegram to Wrigley: "Who stinks now?"

The Cubs struggled after the lost World Series, and reporters joked that Sianis must have put a curse on the team. He went along with it.

Late in 1950, a season in which the Cubs would lose 89 games and finish seventh in the eight-team National League, *Chicago Sun-Times* sports columnist Gene Kessler suggested Sianis write a letter to Wrigley, saying he would remove the curse in exchange for a formal apology. The newspaper printed Wrigley's response: "Will you please extend to [your goat] my sincere apologies...and ask him not only to remove the 'hex' but to reverse the flow and start pulling for wins."

It didn't work. In 1951, the Cubs lost 92 games and finished eighth. And they would not reach the postseason again until 1984.

Grimm, by the way, returned to manage in 1960 but lasted 17 games before he switched places with broadcaster Lou Boudreau. Pafko also played for Grimm when he managed the Milwaukee Braves in the early 1950s and liked his exuberance for the game. Rockwell liked Grimm's face and in 1948 featured the Cubs skipper in the famous painting *The Dugout*. Grimm is seen sitting in the dugout with his head in his hand and obviously not pleased with what was happening on the field.

The artist presented Grimm with a charcoal draft of the painting and signed it: "To Charles Grimm, a long suffering but wonderful manager, Norman Rockwell."

The goat does not appear in either version.

43

PAT HUGHES

About a half hour before the first pitch of a Cubs game at Wrigley Field, radio play-by-play announcer Pat Hughes enters the press box dining room for a quick pregame meal. Craig Lynch is waiting for him.

Hughes' voice helps Lynch see the game. Craig Lynch is blind.

"When he's not at the game," Lynch said, "you miss him."

It's Lynch's connection to Hughes that's the focus of this chapter— but first, a little more about Pat Hughes.

He grew up in Northern California, where he listened to Russ Hodges and Lon Simmons, voices of the San Francisco Giants. At night, Hughes could tune his radio to the Dodgers' games and find the incomparable Vin Scully. Those voices inspired him to become a broadcaster, and after time in Minnesota with the Twins and in Milwaukee with the Brewers, he joined the Cubs' broadcast team in 1996.

He has great respect for the history of baseball, and a special admiration for those who have broadcast the sport over the decades. He created "Baseball Voices," commemorative audio tributes to some of the game's top announcers. His profiles include Hodges, Simmons, longtime radio partner Ron Santo, plus legendary Cubs broadcaster Harry Caray, as well as Mel Allen, Bob Prince, Jack Buck, Marty Brennaman, Harry Kalas, Bob Uecker, Red Barber, Dave Niehaus, and Jon Miller.

After the Cubs won the 2016 World Series, Hughes made a special CD to celebrate the team's first championship in 108 years. Baseball was not broadcast on the radio in 1908, the last time the Cubs won, so Hughes was the first Cubs broadcaster to say, live and on the air, "The Cubs win the World Series."

That's on the disc.

Back to Lynch. Now past 70, he's a freelance journalist. Blind since birth, he would sit in the fourth row of the Wrigley Field press box with a transistor radio pressed against his ear, tuned to the Cubs broadcast.

He and Hughes see the game as one.

"He describes the uniforms," Lynch noted. Hughes is famous for his precise uniform details—"blue pinstripes, blue cap, red trim"—which gives folks listening in downstate Illinois, as well as Lynch, an image. "He's got a certain pattern."

Hughes also is a master at describing what's happening in the actual games.

"Back in 2003, the Cubs had Troy O'Leary, he was an outfielder, and he hit a triple," Lynch said. "Pat described it so well. People used to ask me, 'What do you miss about not seeing?' I found out that day I missed being able to see Troy O'Leary's triple. Pat described it just perfectly."

Close your eyes and try to follow a Cubs game, relying solely on the broadcasters' voices. That's how Lynch watches a game.

Craig Lynch's father took him to his first Cubs game in July 1955, when he was five years old. He remembers sitting in a section in the Wrigley Field grandstand in which WGN television broadcaster Jack Brickhouse's play-by-play was piped in.

"The good thing about baseball is you can follow a baseball game on television or radio," Lynch said. "The only sport a blind person really has trouble following is basketball."

On afternoons when Lynch got out of school, he would listen to the end of the Cubs games on his transistor radio, which he brought to games when he went with his friends. Remember, this was before iPads or Wi-Fi.

Lynch became a regular in the bleachers and was the inspiration for the blind, radio-toting character "Greg" in the stage play *Bleacher Bums*.

"We used to sit in center field, just to the right of the scoreboard," Lynch said. "At that time, there were these elderly men who used to gamble and they would bet on everything. [Actor-director-playwright] Joe Mantegna was there and part of the Organic Theater Company. Unbeknownst to us, these people [from the theater company] were out there one day—they're youngish, in my age bracket or maybe a year or two older. They started talking to us and that's how the play *Bleacher Bums* was written.

"I used to tell corny puns and silly things," Lynch said. "They amplified the character [for the play]."

Lynch and Hughes first met in 1996 in Hughes' first season with partner Santo. Lynch was listening to the radio broadcast and noted that neither Hughes nor Santo had mentioned a player substitution during the game.

"I went over to the booth and popped my head in," Lynch said. "Ron Santo knew who I was. I said, 'So-and-so is playing the outfield now.' Pat mentioned my name on the radio that day and said I'd corrected him. Over the years, we started sitting together at lunch. He likes trivia and he would ask questions. Then he would say, 'Do you guys have any trivia?' The longer it went on, the more I felt I was expected to have trivia questions."

In the press box dining room, Hughes and Lynch are almost always exchanging tidbits about baseball history. Cubs television broadcasters Len Kasper and Jim Deshaies often join in, as does Hughes' current radio partner, Ron Coomer.

"It became something I was expected to do," Lynch said about providing the questions. "Even Jim and Len said on TV, 'We'll have to ask Craig Lynch about it.' And I'm not a trivia expert really. It just kind of evolved, so now I'm expected to have a trivia question every day. I like doing it, so I'll try to get more. Ron Coomer will come in and say, 'Okay, do you have your 'A' game today?'"

For the record, Lynch does listen to the Cubs television broadcasts as well as the radio. Which medium he stays with depends on how the team is doing at that moment. He's a little superstitious.

"For example, if I have the TV on and the radio off and there's a hit, I'll leave the same person broadcasting until they make an out," Lynch said. "When they're losing, I never want to hear the last out of the game. A couple of times I've actually turned the radio off and missed the winning home run. That's okay—I'd rather not hear it and win than hear it and lose. I can get the highlight after.

"I'm not superstitious in life," Lynch said, "but I am in baseball. Oh, my word, it's terrible."

Which Hughes never is.

"I've told him several times what a good listen he is," Lynch said. "I have told him several times on certain home runs that he made a great call.

"That triple that Troy O'Leary hit in 2003—I even asked him, 'How do you go about calling a play like that?' He said, 'First you have to follow the ball, and then you have to follow the runners.'"

That's how Pat Hughes sees it.

And that's how Craig Lynch sees it.

44

ANTHONY RIZZO

Anthony Rizzo has survived a 101-loss season and celebrated a World Series championship. He's danced on the tarp and in the dugout. He's huggable—David Ross calls the first baseman a "big teddy bear"—but won't back down in a tough at-bat. Rizzo has been in the middle of the Cubs' batting order since he arrived in 2012, except for those few times he was inserted into the leadoff spot.

However, his biggest moments have come off the field.

Theo Epstein, then the Cubs' president of baseball operations, knew exactly who he was getting when he traded for the first baseman in January 2012. Epstein was with the Red Sox in 2007 when he drafted Rizzo in the sixth round. He had a bright future as an 18-year-old minor leaguer in 2008. But in April that year, his life was turned upside down when he was diagnosed with limited stage classical Hodgkin's lymphoma.

Rizzo's grandmother was dealing with breast cancer at the same time. His parents were frightened. But Rizzo was fortunate and returned to play baseball in 2009. He never forgot the fear his family felt and it inspired him to create the Anthony Rizzo Family Foundation (ARFF) to help cancer patients and their families.

"I always say my parents went through it worse than I did, so if I can, I talk to the parents, and say, 'It's harder for you guys than it is for the kid, and everything will be okay,'" Rizzo told me. "I say the same thing to the kids. I tell them, 'Your parents feel worse than you do.'"

The foundation, created in 2012, has hosted walk-a-thons, food events, and comedy fundraisers to provide grants for families facing financial hardship resulting from a child's treatment for cancer. ARFF also supports oncology child life specialists, whose duties include explaining treatment to anxious parents and their children.

Rizzo may be an All-Star and a key piece of the Cubs' success, but when he walks onto the 18th floor at the Ann & Robert H. Lurie Children's Hospital in Chicago, he switches from being a big-league ballplayer to

Anthony Rizzo celebrated after catching the final out of Game 7 of the 2016 World Series. "You've got to have fun," said the cancer survivor. "We only have a short window to play this game."

just Anthony. He'll meet with young cancer patients and try to ease their fears and worries.

Those moments are precious. Rizzo shares how he played games on his Xbox, drank milkshakes, and ate brownies to deal with chemotherapy. To this day, he avoids drinking red Gatorade because when he underwent chemo, he received a red injection that looked like the sports drink and it made him nauseous. He can relate to nervous young patients.

"He would never tell us how much it hurt," Anthony's father, John, told me. "He'd always tell us, 'Don't worry about it, it's fine, it's fine.' But the chemo was killing him. He went through it pretty well. He always had a great attitude."

The Rizzo foundation's motto is "Stay Strong, Dream Big," and its efforts have been successful. In 2017, ARFF donated $3.5 million to Lurie Children's Hospital, and a waiting room was named in Rizzo's honor. The foundation also presented money to the Sylvester Comprehensive Cancer Center at the University of Miami Health system, where Rizzo received treatment.

When he visits patients, Rizzo does so without any fanfare.

"I don't go in there to let people know I had cancer," he told me. "When I do tell people, it's a personal thing. They're going through it, I've been through it. I know I can relate. I know exactly what their parents are going through because I saw my parents go through it."

Rizzo hosts his "Walk-Off for Cancer" at Pine Trails Park in his hometown of Parkland, Florida, which is where he found himself on February 15, 2018, to speak to the community at a candlelight vigil after a tragic shooting at his alma mater, Marjory Stoneman Douglas High School. Seventeen people were killed, and Rizzo knew some of the victims.

"I'm a baseball player, but I'm also an American," Rizzo said that night through tears. "I'm a Floridian and a Parklander for life. While I don't have all the answers, I know something has to change before this is visited on another community and another community and another community."

Rizzo has dealt with enough life-or-death moments that going 0-for-4 in a game isn't the end of the world. During the pandemic in 2020, his foundation shifted gears and rallied to serve meals to healthcare workers at 30 different hospitals in six different states.

KING KELLY

If you ever got an autograph from a major league player, you can thank King Kelly.

Michael Joseph "King" Kelly played for the Cubs before they were the Cubs. From 1880 to '86, he was a star on the Chicago White Stockings, the precursor to the Cubs, although he joined the team in an unusual way. Kelly was playing for the Cincinnati Reds in 1879, but the team reportedly lost $10,000, which was a huge sum at the time. Owner J. Wayne Neff released all of the players, saying he couldn't pay them.

Kelly went on a barnstorming trip with some other players, including Cap Anson, then the captain of the White Stockings. Anson liked what he saw and asked Kelly to join the Chicago team.

"He was a whole-souled, genial fellow, with a host of friends, and but one enemy, that one being himself," Anson said of Kelly in his biography, *A Ball Player's Career.*

The problem? Kelly drank. A lot. Despite that, he compiled a .316 batting average in his seven seasons in Chicago, winning the batting title in 1886 with a major league–leading .388 average. (The other major league that year was the American Association. Among its players: Cyclone Miller, Toad Ramsey, Sadie Houck, Blondie Purcell, and Charlie Comiskey—the young "Old Roman"—who hit .254 for the St. Louis Browns.) The White Stockings won the National League pennant in five of his seven years there.

A handsome man who sported a full mustache, Kelly was creative. Anson gave Kelly credit for originating the hit-and-run play. Kelly also got his teammates to adjust their outfield defense, depending on the batter, and the White Stockings employed an infield shift at times.

Kelly did take some liberties. He stole at least 50 bases in four consecutive years, and occasionally took advantage of the umpire when his back was turned to run from second to home and avoid third base completely.

"Kelly, in his day, was as popular a figure as Babe Ruth would later be, and there was hardly a boy in the land who did not follow the daily doings of the King," according to Lee Allen, a historian with the national Baseball Hall of Fame.

However, Chicago team owner A.J. Spalding would not acquiesce to Kelly's salary demands after the 1886 season and released him, which the outfielder called "the kindest action of his life." In February 1887, Boston signed him for $10,000.

"Kelly has had the Captain bee in his bonnet for a long time and hoped to become chief of the Chicago club," Spalding told the *Chicago Tribune.* "I think he was discouraged at the outlook, and that possibly added to his discontent. He may be able to do better for himself in his new place, and we shall see him often enough not to forget how he looks and plays."

Kelly made it clear he was happy with the move.

"Some time ago Spalding said that I would have to eat grass if I didn't play with his club," Kelly told reporters. "In order to remind him of his statement I wrote, 'Mr. Spalding, I shall eat strawberry shortcake this summer,' and mailed it with my photograph."

Kelly was more than a ballplayer; he was a celebrity. He was seen about town and never shied away from a reporter. Upon Kelly's arrival in Boston, fans would follow him around town and ask for him to sign his name on a piece of paper. Although he wasn't the first to do so, Kelly is credited with popularizing autographs.

He was the first to author an autobiography—*Play Ball: Stories of the Ball Field*—and the first to have a hit song—"Slide, Kelly, Slide"—written about him. He would recite "Casey at the Bat" on stage. He received extra income from endorsements, including a Kelly-brand shoe polish.

Chicago fans were bitter about his departure, and some refused to attend the season opener in 1887.

"Kelly was a general on the diamond, a born humorist, and an agreeable companion," Anson told the *Chicago Tribune* at the time of Kelly's death. "As a batter and baserunner, Mike had few equals, and no man was ever of more value behind the bat. Contrary to the general opinion, he was not a hard man to get along with, and I would willingly have had him on the Chicago team at any time."

Even if Kelly had difficulties managing himself, he did love the game and devoted himself to it.

"Friends advised me to go to work and leave base ball alone," Kelly wrote in his book. "They predicted that it would ruin me. Friends are sometimes wrong. Never disappoint a boy, parents, if you wish him to be successful in this world. If he wishes to be a clergyman, do not change his mind. He may be a heart-broken, disappointed man in later years.

"...If he wishes to become a base ball player, encourage him to be an honest one. There is honor in every profession. 'Tis an honor to be an honest ball player."

Kelly played a total of 16 seasons, finished in 1893 with the New York Giants, and wound up with a .307 career average. The next year, he was dead, of pneumonia.

"King" Kelly was 36 years old.

His attitude was just what the Cubs needed during the bizarre, abbreviated 2020 season.

"He's one of the best competitors I've been around," Ross said of the first baseman. "He's got that love and infectious personality. He wants everybody to have a good time. He's really embraced this environment and the team concept, which I've always seen.

"He knows how to have a good time and knows how to play the game with passion and focus, which is a unique skill set and I know how hard it is. Even when he doesn't have a good at-bat, or gave away an at-bat, he's mad for a second and turns back around and starts cheering for the guy behind him."

As cliché as it sounds, Rizzo will do whatever it takes to win, even if it means leading off. The first time he led off in June 2017, he launched the second pitch of the game from the Mets' Zack Wheeler for a home run. Rizzo reached safely in each of his first seven games leading off, hitting home runs in three of those. The next year, Cubs manager Joe Maddon briefly inserted Rizzo into the No. 1 spot again, and he compiled a .439 on-base percentage from July 13 to August 14.

The Cubs' preference is to have Rizzo in position where he can choke up on the bat and drive in runs. He has delivered. Rizzo totaled at least 100 RBIs in four consecutive seasons (2015–18) and is the first left-handed batter to do so in Cubs history. He excelled in the field as well, winning multiple Gold Gloves, making acrobatic catches, and learning how to deal with obstacles like a tarp as well as the wind at Wrigley Field.

Take a game on August 12, 2015, when the Brewers' Ryan Braun hit a pop-up toward the first-base side at Wrigley Field. Rizzo jumped onto the rolled tarp there, then stepped on top of the brick wall and then the back of a seat. He held onto the ball as he landed on his feet amid cheering fans and had the presence of mind to throw the ball back to the infield.

"It's a really dangerous play, obviously," Braun said. "You have no idea where you're going to land. If his foot were to hit the seat wrong or fall in-between seats, he could have broken an ankle. So for him to even attempt that, it's a special play by a really good player."

When Maddon was hired as the Cubs' manager, he dined with Rizzo before spring training began.

"From him to me, I got that he was pretty mature for his age and a guy who understands his role within this organization and within the game of baseball," Maddon said. "I think he understands the bigger picture, too. He wants to win, and he's a guy who embraces a more free-spirited approach to life and the game."

Free spirit? When the Cubs were down three games to one in the 2016 World Series, Rizzo did a pregame dance in the clubhouse to the theme music from the movie *Rocky*. In the dugout, he quoted Burgess Meredith's character, Mickey, before his at-bats. The Cubs won.

In the Cubs' first game of the pandemic-delayed 2020 season, Rizzo carried a small bottle of hand sanitizer in the back pocket of his uniform and offered some to Orlando Arcia after the Brewers' infielder had reached first.

After Starlin Castro was traded, Rizzo paid homage to his former teammate during the Cubs' home opener in 2016 by using Castro's lively walk-up music, "Ando En La Versace" by Omega, for his first at-bat. That always seemed to rev up the crowd at Wrigley Field, and fans—and teammates in the dugout—clapped along.

"You've got to have fun," Rizzo said. "We only have a short window to play this game. Everyone in here has fun, and that's what the game is all about.

"It's just like when we were kids."

45

PHIL CAVARRETTA

Imagine being a young boy in Chicago and your high school coach arranges a tryout with the Cubs. The boy knows all about the team. He used to go to Wrigley Field to help clean up after games, stuffing a burlap bag with trash collected in the stands. Doing so was worth it because he got a free ticket for the next home game.

The kid was a star pitcher and first baseman for Lane Tech's 1933 city championship team, although at that time, the school was known as the Albert Grannis Lane Manual Training High School and located at Division and Sedgwick Streets, well away from its present location—less than two miles from Wrigley Field.

Baseball was foreign to his parents, who were immigrants from Palermo, Sicily. They spoke Italian at home.

The Cubs staff was a little confused at the tryout. The youngster looked more like a bat boy than a potential prospect, because though approaching 6'0", he only weighed about 150 pounds.

But he impressed them during the workout and was offered a contract. He signed and was assigned to a Class B minor league team in Peoria. He hadn't finished high school yet and his father was opposed to giving up books for baseball, but the Cubs were going to pay him $125 a month—this was during the Depression—and he was going to send half of that home to his family.

In his first minor league game on May 15, 1934, he hit for the cycle. Less than three months later, he was called up to the Cubs, and in his first at-bat in his first start at Wrigley Field on September 25, he hit a game-winning home run in a 1–0 win against the Reds.

He had just turned 18 years old.

There should have been a movie about Phil Cavarretta's path to the Cubs.

"I was blessed with ability," Cavarretta told me. "The good Lord says he'll put you on earth to become a professional baseball player, and he says it's going to be up to you to play hard and be successful. That's the truth. That's why I always gave 110 percent."

His effort paid off. Cavarretta batted .293 in his 22-year career, playing all but his final two seasons with the Cubs. (He finished up with the crosstown White Sox.) He was exempt from military service because he had a perforated eardrum, but the hearing problem didn't affect his play. In 1945, Cavarretta won the National League batting title and was named the league's Most Valuable Player.

"It was the kind of year you dream of," Cavarretta said of that season. "Everything has to go your way, your line drives have to drop, your broken-bat hits have to drop."

"Philibuck" (the nickname was courtesy of his first manager, Charlie Grimm) was a tough ballplayer and an honest manager, and that honesty cost him his job. Prior to the start of his fourth season as skipper in 1954, Cavarretta was fired during spring training after he told owner Phil Wrigley that the Cubs most likely wouldn't finish above fifth place.

"Phil has the fighting spirit and likes to win," Wrigley told the Associated Press in March 1954. "But this year when he picked everyone but us to finish in the first division, he was licked before he started. He said he did not have the kind of ballplayers he wanted. He had sort of given up on the boys, so to speak, feeling that they were not pennant material.

"Well, maybe not, but they could be with the will to win. I've seen pennants won by teams that were not much on paper but they won anyway. It even happened to us once."

Stan Hack took over for Cavarretta, who turned out to be correct: the '54 Cubs finished seventh.

Cavarretta played in three World Series with the Cubs (1935, '38, and '45) but never won the championship. He shared his love of the game with his son, Phil Jr., who would get a history lesson every time they watched the Cubs together on television.

"Being a ballplayer, he sees the game in a way other people don't," Phil Jr. told me. "There's 100 times I've disagreed with him, and he ends up being right. On the younger players, he'll say, 'He can't hit this and that.' And he knows."

In 2003, Phil Jr.'s son Matthew waited until the last minute to try to get tickets for Game 5 of the National League Division Series between the Cubs and Braves in Atlanta.

In his first major league start in September 1934, Phil Cavarretta homered in his first at-bat for the game-winner. He was 18. (Getty Images)

"He brought my dad's baseball card, brought it for luck," Phil Jr. said. "There was a Cub fan selling tickets outside Turner Field, and a Braves fan wanted to buy them. My son says, 'My grandfather played for the Cubs' and showed the card."

The Cubs won that game, clinching their first postseason series since 1908. And Phil Cavarretta's grandson—though he didn't have to stuff a burlap bag with trash to do it—got the tickets.

46

JON LESTER

They had watched Jon Lester develop in the minor leagues, supported him during his battle with cancer in 2006, and cheered for him when he pitched for the Red Sox. In 2014, Theo Epstein and Jed Hoyer had shifted from running the Boston franchise to Chicago. Could they woo Lester, a free agent, to join the Cubs in their rebuilding efforts?

Epstein, president of baseball operations, and Hoyer, the general manager, didn't waste time. On the first day of free agency in November 2014, Lester received a package that included Cubs hats and shirts in camouflage design—the pitcher's favorite—plus some bottles of fine wine.

There also was a slick 15-minute DVD that ended with Lester on the mound to get the last out of the World Series and Cubs players rushing to celebrate. It was titled: *How the Cubs Are Going to Win a World Series with Jon Lester in 2015 and Beyond.*

When Lester and his wife, Farrah, visited Wrigley Field, they were briefed on the renovation plans for the ballpark, how the Cubs would support their NVRQT Foundation ("Never Quit," devoted to pediatric cancer research), and increased family time because they played in the travel-friendly Central Division.

Epstein highlighted the young talent on the Cubs roster—Kris Bryant, Javier Baez, Kyle Schwarber, and Anthony Rizzo. Lester knew Rizzo. The two had met when Rizzo was a Red Sox minor leaguer and had been diagnosed with Hodgkin's lymphoma. Lester had dealt with the same cancer and beaten it.

Cubs owner Tom Ricketts and Lester dined in downtown Chicago and talked about hunting. Epstein may have never gone hunting with Lester while they were together in Boston, but he was willing to do anything to persuade the pitcher to sign with the Cubs.

Some hunters use urine to lure deer within range.

"I was ready to soak myself in deer urine if necessary," Epstein said, "but I didn't have to."

"I'll take him hunting, but we're not going to do the deer urine," Lester quipped.

The top free-agent pitcher on the market that offseason, Lester was courted by the Giants, who sent catcher Buster Posey to visit; and the Red Sox, who had dealt Lester to Oakland in mid-2014 but who now hoped second baseman Dustin Pedroia could persuade the lefty to return.

The Cubs made their final offer. Another team tempted Lester with more money, but Lester had already won two World Series with the Red Sox; here was a chance to do something historic in Chicago. Epstein's relationship with the pitcher and the Cubs' bright future helped seal the deal.

Joe Maddon was at dinner in San Diego during the winter meetings when he got a text message from Epstein that Lester was on board. Maddon had only been on the job as Cubs manager for a couple months. As he entered the lobby of the headquarters hotel, he was approached by reporters trying to confirm the Lester rumors.

"It's not often you get to win the lottery," Maddon said.

Lester agreed to a six-year, $155 million deal, the largest in Cubs history. It might be the best free-agent signing ever by the team.

"It doesn't happen every day—a player taking less, let alone to a team that finished in last place," Epstein said. "I think it emphasizes how much he wanted to be here and the fact that he came here for the right reasons, which was important to us."

What the signing did—and why it's pertinent—is that it sent a message to Cubs fans that after years of rebuilding, they now were serious about contending. This was a pitcher with a stellar track record who had won World Series rings. The message: it was not a question of if the Cubs would win a World Series but when.

"This signing really marks a transition of sorts for the Cubs, the start of a period where we are clearly very serious about bringing a World Series to the Cubs and the people of Chicago," Epstein said. "It's a great day for our fans. They've been so patient with us, incredibly patient, over the last few years, and they truly deserve a pitcher and a person of this caliber to call their own."

Lester got his own message that he made the right decision shortly after he arrived in Arizona for spring training in February 2015. He recorded his first hole-in-one during his first round of golf for the year.

Lester did just what Epstein hoped he would do, although it took one extra year. In 2016, Lester was 19–5 with a 2.44 ERA, won three of his five postseason starts, and chipped in to pitch in relief in Game 7 of the World Series, helping the Cubs win the championship.

So the DVD didn't get it quite right—Lester didn't get the final out, and it was Mike Montgomery who got mobbed. But without Lester, there would be no Cubs rushing to the mound to celebrate.

"The biggest thing that made me believe in the Cubs was Jed and Theo," Lester said. "They made me believe in what they believe in."

47

GABBY HARTNETT

He hit one of the most memorable home runs in Cubs franchise history and had a front-row seat for another.

Discovered while playing for the Worcester Boosters of the Class A Eastern League, Charles Leo Hartnett—dubbed Gabby when he first joined the team because he was just the opposite—reported to Cubs spring training on Catalina Island in 1922. Chicago manager Bill Killefer tested the rookie right away by having Hartnett catch Grover Cleveland Alexander, and the veteran right-hander praised the youngster. That was enough for the Cubs, although Hartnett spent that season backing up catcher Bob O'Farrell.

In 1924, O'Farrell was injured and Hartnett took over, batting .299 with 16 home runs in 111 games. He finished tied for 15th in the Most Valuable Player voting (and would eventually win the award in 1935). It became Hartnett's job full time when O'Farrell was traded in May 1925, but the season ended badly for both Hartnett and his team: in the last game, Hartnett dropped a pop fly, which allowed two runs to score, handing the Cubs the loss and a last-place finish for the first time in franchise history. However, that also meant they had the first pick in the minor league draft—and it paid off when the Cubs selected Hack Wilson, who would enjoy a Hall of Fame career.

Hartnett caught 100 or more games in 12 seasons, including eight years in a row. In 1934, he was the National League's starting catcher in the All-Star Game and caught Giants pitcher Carl Hubbell when he struck out Babe Ruth, Lou Gehrig, and Jimmie Foxx in the first inning, then Al Simmons and Joe Cronin to open the second. Yankees manager Joe McCarthy called Hartnett "the perfect catcher."

But it's those home runs that were special.

In 1932, the Yankees had won the first two games of the World Series against the Cubs and their vaunted pitching staff, which boasted the lowest ERA in the NL. Game 3 was tied at 4 with one out in the top of the fifth at Wrigley Field when Ruth stepped in to face Charlie Root, who got ahead 0–2 against the Yankee slugger.

According to *Chicago Tribune* reporter Irving Vaughan, Guy Bush and Bob Smith were leaning out of the Cubs' dugout and razzing Ruth during the at-bat.

"That's only two strikes, boys. I still have one coming," Ruth reportedly responded, holding up two fingers and pointing toward the outfield.

Ruth then launched the next pitch to "distant parts," as Vaughan wrote. Lou Gehrig followed with another homer off Root, and the Yankees would win 7–5 and go on to sweep the Series.

"It was a change of pace ball, low outside," Root said of Ruth's shot. "If it had been a fastball I wouldn't have been surprised. But he picked out a slow curve and sent it on a line to center. That convinced me of the tremendous power he has in his swings."

Did Ruth call it? Hartnett didn't think so.

"There were two strikes on Babe," Hartnett told *Chicago Tribune* columnist Dave Condon. "He waved his hand across the plate toward the Cub bench on the third base side. One finger was up. At the same time he said softly, 'It only takes one to hit it.' I think only the umpire and myself heard him say it.

"Babe didn't say a word when he passed me after the home run. If he had pointed at the bleachers, I'd be the first to say so. We tried every kind of pitch on Ruth in that Series. It didn't make any difference. There'll never be another like him."

On September 28, 1938, Hartnett hit a home run that had a better result for the Cubs.

He'd taken over as manager in July that year, replacing Charlie Grimm, and the Cubs, after winning the opener of the three-game series with Pittsburgh at Wrigley Field, were a half game behind the first-place Pirates heading into Game 2.

The game was tied at 5 after eight innings, and it was getting dark. Remember, Wrigley wouldn't get lights for another 50 years. The umpires had decided they'd play one more inning. At that time, suspended games were not resumed, so if the game stayed tied, the two teams would have to play a doubleheader the next day.

With one out in the top of the ninth, the Pirates' Paul Waner singled—but one out later, Hartnett threw him out trying to steal second to end the inning.

Pittsburgh's Mace Brown retired the first two Cubs batters in the home ninth and was ahead 0–2 to Hartnett after throwing two fastballs. Brown then threw a high curve that Hartnett drove to left center, although not many of the 34,465 at Wrigley could see it.

"I swung with everything I had, and then I got that feeling, the kind of feeling you get when the blood rushes out of your head and you get dizzy," Hartnett said.

"A lot of people have told me they didn't know the ball was in the bleachers. Well, I did. Maybe I was the only one in the park who did. I knew the moment I hit it. I don't think I saw third base...and I don't think I walked a step to the plate—I was carried in."

The "Homer in the Gloamin'" is one of the signature walk-off homers of all time. The Cubs crushed the Pirates 10–1 the next day to complete a sweep and cap a 10-game winning streak.

"The greatest thrill of my life," Hartnett said.

The Yankees, however, swept the Cubs again in the World Series.

The Cubs finished fifth in 1940, and Hartnett was dismissed as manager. He played part time for the New York Giants in 1941 and then retired, eventually opening a bowling alley and sporting goods store just outside Chicago in Lincolnwood, Illinois. Born on December 20, 1900, in Woonsocket, Rhode Island, Gabby Hartnett died 72 years later on the same day.

Inducted into the Hall of Fame in 1955, he enjoyed his status as the "Homer in the Gloamin'" catcher. Once, while pheasant hunting, his companions noticed that he didn't miss many targets.

"I'm hitting 'em well today because it's so dark," Hartnett told the *Tribune*'s Dave Condon in January 1968. "As they said at the Old Timers' dinner, I always was at my best when I couldn't see."

48

DAVID ROSS

It wasn't that David Ross had forever dreamed of managing the Cubs.

But he had started thinking about managing—managing somewhere—long before October 2019, when president of baseball operations Theo Epstein offered him the opportunity to be the Cubs' next skipper. When you total more than 200 at-bats in a single season only twice in a 15-year career, and you're a reserve catcher, and you love the game, you spend a lot of time on the bench watching and learning.

And David Ross spent a lot of time watching and learning from some of the best, including Bobby Cox, Terry Francona, John Farrell, and Joe Maddon.

Ross came to the Cubs in 2015 as a free-agent backup catcher, about to turn 38, coming off a season with Boston when he'd hit .184. In his first year as a Cub, he hit .176 with one home run in 159 at-bats.

But for a variety of reasons, veteran Ross became veteran Jon Lester's personal catcher—and in two years evolved into the fan favorite "Grandpa Rossy."

In the sixth inning of Game 7 of the 2016 World Series, he homered off the Indians' Andrew Miller to pad a Cubs lead—a lead they would lose. But when the Cubs finally won 8–7 in 10 innings to capture their first World Series since even before Ross was born, the players hoisted Grandpa onto their shoulders.

"I hit a home run in Game 7 and I got carried off the field," Ross said. "That doesn't happen. It's like *Rudy*."

And then he retired.

"It's time," Ross said. "I don't want to be that guy who stays at the party too long."

He didn't disappear. He joined the Cubs' front office as a special assistant. He offered insights as a baseball analyst on ESPN. His newfound celebrity status gave him a chance to be the first-ever light-hitting (.229 lifetime) catcher to twirl in sequins as a contestant on *Dancing with the Stars*. (He and a partner—evidently Lester was unavailable—finished second to a running back.)

Then he got that dream job.

"I've had an eye on this my entire career," Ross said.

What he—and the rest of the world—did not anticipate was a pandemic that shut down Major League Baseball in the middle of spring training in March 2020 and delayed the start of the season more than 3½ months. Ross later joked that there were no questions from Epstein during the interview process about COVID-19 safety protocols.

But to David Ross, playing a shortened season wouldn't cheapen the prize.

"If they're passing out a trophy, I want it," he quipped, which, these being the Cubs, instantly became a T-shirt slogan.

As Ross' playing career squatted to a finish, teammates Anthony Rizzo and Kris Bryant created an Instagram account to document Ross' farewell tour. Outfielder Jason Heyward, who first met Ross when the two were teammates on the Braves, paid for the veteran to have a hotel suite on the road, instead of a simple room, the entire 2016 season. In spring training, the Cubs presented Ross with a shiny red motorized cart to help him get around the practice facility.

This—in a year that would be historic on the North Side—was a team with a sense of history.

"The guy never ceases to amaze me," Lester said of his catcher. "We're talking about—and not a knock on him—but we're talking about a backup catcher and the impact he had on these guys here and has had on me.

"There's not many guys in this game when you're done who you still keep in contact with. He's definitely one of them for me."

What Lester didn't know in 2016 was that he and Ross would still be in contact in 2020 but in a much different context.

None of the Cubs' players, not even Lester, could know which David Ross they would get as their new manager. Would it be the lovable and self-deprecating Grandpa Rossy? Or the catcher who wasn't afraid to yell at Lester on the mound?

"I know there's a big, fun-loving 'Grandpa Rossy' theme out there," Ross said when introduced as the Cubs' manager, "but if you ask any of my friends or ex-players what kind of teammate I was, I didn't shy away from the tough conversations.

"If I would've been mic'd up for some of those conversations on the mound, they were rarely friendly conversations. To the core, I'm a guy who has a lot of expectations when I come into work. I'm very professional, I expect professionalism and those traits I talked about—the effort and accountability—I don't shy away from those conversations."

On July 24, 2020, Kyle Hendricks threw a complete game in a 3–0 win over the Brewers at Wrigley Field. Ross did go out to the mound with two outs in the ninth to check on Hendricks but left the right-hander in to finish, prompting applause from the Cubs players in the dugout. What he didn't hear, in a ballpark kept fanless by the pandemic, was a roar from a crowd that, in normal times, would have shaken the ancient rafters.

"They said the only reason I was going out there was to get a cheer," Ross said. "So, they gave it to me on the way back. There's no fans in there to [yell], 'Let him stay in.' I just wanted to go check his pulse."

Hendricks needed just one more pitch to end the game. Ross got a game ball and the lineup card as souvenirs from his first major league win as a manager as well as hundreds of text messages.

"I love that guy," Hendricks said of Ross. "And we just love playing for him."

49

GAME 5 NLDS AND WADE DAVIS

Cubs manager Joe Maddon wanted spring training 2017 to be business as usual and dismissed talk of any hangover from the team's historic 2016 World Series championship. The next step was to prove 2016 wasn't a fluke.

Aroldis Chapman, who was the Cubs' second-half closer in '16 and a decisive addition, had rejoined the Yankees. The Cubs acquired right-hander Wade Davis from the Royals to take his place.

If there were any hints of a hangover, it would be up to Davis to provide the relief. And nowhere would the cure be more emphatic than in Game 5 of the 2017 National League Division Series.

Maddon knew Davis from their days together on the Rays (2009–12). He had been converted from starter to reliever by the Royals in 2014; when Kansas City manager Ned Yost had asked Davis to move to the bullpen, the pitcher's response was exactly what he needed to hear.

"Wade looked at me and said, 'Skip, I don't care what I do. If it's starting rotation, if it's the bullpen, I just want to be the best at what I do,'" Yost told me. "From that point on, in my mind, if he wasn't the best, he was certainly one of the top three relievers in the game."

Pitching in relief seemed to benefit Davis. Both the Royals and the Cubs noticed an uptick in his velocity in those instances. Not exactly, Davis said.

"It's not like I gained these velocity gains," Davis said in spring training 2017. "It just became more consistent. I think I got better because I got bigger and stronger and started working harder."

What made Davis even more special was his fearlessness.

"There were times when you think there'd be no way that Wade would get out of a situation," Yost said. "There was no situation too big for him. He always found ways."

The Cubs were challenged that season and trailed the Brewers by 5½ games at the All-Star break, but they overcame injuries and got contributions from players including Javier Baez and Willson Contreras to rally in the second half and repeat as Central Division champs. Next up were the Nationals in the NL Division Series.

Davis was needed to extend himself for one of the Cubs' biggest moments.

The right-hander picked up saves in the Cubs' wins in Games 1 and 3 in the NLDS. He also pitched in Game 4, a 5–0 Washington win in which the Cubs used six pitchers. The best-of-five series was tied at two wins apiece to set up Game 5 at Nationals Park.

The Nationals took a 4–1 lead in the second inning against starter Kyle Hendricks, but the Cubs countered with two in the third, then scored four runs in the fifth against ace Max Scherzer to go ahead 7–4.

Cubs reliever Carl Edwards Jr. had pitched in all four games of the series and took the mound in the seventh with the Cubs ahead 9–6, but he walked the first batter he faced. Maddon called upon Jose Quintana, who had started Game 3. The Nationals added a run to pull within 9–7. That's when Davis entered, and he struck out Ryan Zimmerman to end the inning.

But Davis' night wasn't over. The Cubs' pitchers were gassed. Davis walked the first two batters in the eighth, then got pinch-hitter Adam Lind to ground into a double play. Michael A. Taylor hit an RBI single, but Davis got a huge assist from Contreras, who picked off Jose Lobaton at first base to end the inning. Lobaton was originally called safe and the Cubs challenged the ruling. After a review, it was overturned.

Out came Davis for the ninth. If he glanced at the visitors' bullpen, he would have seen no one was warming up. This was his game.

He got Trea Turner to fly out, then struck out Jayson Werth. Davis then struck out Nationals superstar Bryce Harper to end the game and clinch the series.

"I was just trying to stay relaxed," Davis said about Harper's at-bat. "He took such an aggressive swing the first swing that I was hoping he'd stay aggressive. Up to the last pitch, he was still pretty aggressive."

"This game was probably more surreal from start to finish than any other game," Cubs president of baseball operations Theo Epstein said. "Our guys did an unbelievable job of finding a way to gut through it."

It was a gutsy performance by Davis, who threw a season-high 44 pitches.

"He's stone cold. He doesn't have a heartbeat," Cubs first baseman Anthony Rizzo said of Davis. "He goes out there, does his thing and lays it all on the line."

Davis had never recorded a save of four or more outs in his regular season career.

"The guy really just shows up," said the Cubs' Ben Zobrist, a teammate of his at Tampa Bay. "When you extend a closer that long, he has to get up a couple different times like that and try to shut down a hot team that's really coming back in the game, it was a very tough moment. He really hung tough there for us and pulled it out for us."

Once again, in a big situation: Wade Davis found a way.

"GO CUBS GO"

It originated as a song to be played prior to Cubs broadcasts on WGN Radio and evolved into a bouncy postgame celebration that fans sing in Wrigleyville following a win. Steve Goodman would be dazzled to see how his love song "Go Cubs Go" has become as much a part of Wrigley Field's lore as the ivy-covered outfield walls.

The only downside, according to some former Cubs players, is that they can't get their kids to stop singing it.

Goodman began going to Cubs games when he was eight years old. He showed his devotion to the team with his song "Dying Cub Fan's Last Request," but general manager Dallas Green didn't like it because he thought the lyrics were too negative.

Lyrics including...well, these:

> *Do they still play the blues in Chicago*
> *When baseball season rolls around?*
> *When the snow melts away, do the Cubbies still play*
> *In their ivy-covered burial ground?*
> *When I was a boy, they were my pride and joy*
> *But now they only bring fatigue*
> *To the home of the brave, the land of the free*
> *And the doormat of the National League*

Dan Fabian, then the program director and head of promotions at WGN Radio, was looking for a more contemporary song to play before the broadcast. Fabian had considered asking Jimmy Buffett for a Wrigleyville version of "Margaritaville." But then he heard Goodman being interviewed by WGN Radio's Roy Leonard in February 1984 about the Cubs, and Fabian asked the songwriter if he could create something appropriate.

Goodman delivered. When Fabian heard "Go Cubs Go," he said it "flat out blew us away." WGN Radio used the song during the '84 season, which turned out to be a successful year for the team as it rolled to the National League East title.

The Cubs had asked Goodman to sing the national anthem for Game 1 of the NL Championship Series against the Padres, but the songwriter died of leukemia on September 20, 1984, four days before the team clinched the division. He was just 36.

Buffett, who was Goodman's close friend, did the honors instead, saying, "This is for Steve Goodman" before he began.

"It may be my greatest baseball memory," Buffett said. "I believe his spirit truly was at Wrigley Field that day."

The Cubs won 13–0.

However, Goodman's magic couldn't carry the Cubs in the NLCS that year, as they lost to the Padres in five games.

Buffett, who recorded a few of Goodman's songs, including "Banana Republics," was the first artist to play a concert at Wrigley Field in September 2005. During the first show, Buffett stopped playing, stepped to the microphone, and yelled, "What would Stevie Goodman say about this?"

The crowd roared.

But it wasn't until 2007 that fans heard "Go Cubs Go" after wins at Wrigley Field. Jay Blunk, then the director of marketing and sales for the team, came up with the idea and presented it to Bob Vorwald, WGN-TV's director of production. The catch was that TV broadcasters Len Kasper and Bob Brenly were asked to be quiet while the song played. Vorwald said the positive feedback from fans was amazing.

"When the decision was made to try 'Go Cubs Go' as a victory song in 2007, it was based on the rich historical impact the song had with the organization," said Blunk, who worked in the Cubs' marketing department for 22 years before joining the Chicago Blackhawks NHL team.

"The song had been a part of the Cubs landscape for many years, including Cubs radio broadcasts on WGN Radio," Blunk told me. "I always felt the song had depth, more like an anthem that unified the spirit of Chicago and the Cubs. And, when we spoke with WGN television and Bob Vorwald about their thoughts, they sprinkled their magic dust on their coverage of fans singing in unison, fists in the air, arms around each other after every victory. The legend of the song exploded.

"The organic nature of the fan engagement leaves a lot of opportunity for brand advancement—natural, authentic, and meaningful," Blunk said. "It's a sure sign of the true brilliance of Steve Goodman's masterpiece. The fans deserve the credit for making the song something of folklore. We just opened the door for them."

Kasper and Brenly were willing participants.

"People were singing along, and Len and Bob [Brenly] were great because we're like, 'We're going to ask you to be quiet for a little bit here' and they're like, 'Okay, fine,'" Vorwald told me. "A lot of announcers want to do the totals and keep talking. Len and Bob were like, 'No, no, we're fine.' We started showing it and we were getting notes—'Please keep doing that, I sing along at home.' It kind of took on a life of its own. That's the good ideas—they just kind of happen."

Goodman's mother Minette enjoyed it as much as Cubs fans did.

"It blows my mind," she told the *Chicago Tribune* in September 2007. "The Cubs win a game and I get to hear my kid sing again. It's rewarding and comforting at the same time."

In case you want to sing along after Cubs wins, here are the lyrics to Goodman's "Go Cubs Go":

> *Baseball season's underway*
> *Well you better get ready for a brand new day*
> *Hey, Chicago, what do you say*
> *The Cubs are gonna win today*
> *They're singing*
> *Go, Cubs, go*
> *Go, Cubs, go*
> *Hey, Chicago, what do you say*
> *The Cubs are gonna win today*
> *Go, Cubs, go*
> *Go, Cubs, go*
> *Hey, Chicago, what do you say*
> *The Cubs are gonna win today*
> *They got the power, they got the speed*
> *To be the best in the National League*
> *Well this is the year and the Cubs are real*

CHICAGO CUBS

So come on down to Wrigley Field
We're singing now
Go, Cubs, go
Go, Cubs, go
Hey, Chicago, what do you say
The Cubs are gonna win today
Go, Cubs, go
Go, Cubs, go
Hey, Chicago, what do you say
The Cubs are gonna win today.
Baseball time is here again
You can catch it all on WGN
So stamp your feet and clap your hands
Chicago Cubs got the greatest fans
Hear 'em singing now
Go, Cubs, go
Go, Cubs, go
Hey, Chicago, what do you say
The Cubs are gonna win today
Go, Cubs, go
Go, Cubs, go
Hey, Chicago, what do you say
The Cubs are gonna win today

[Acknowledgments]

Picking just 50 Cubs moments wasn't easy. There were at least 50 highlights during the 2016 season alone, capped by the dramatic victory over the Indians in Game 7 of the World Series.

One of my favorite memories of that season came afterward. The championship finally theirs after all those decades of waiting and suffering, Cubs fans scribbled the names of friends and relatives in chalk on Wrigley Field's outside walls. Many of those names represented people—grandparents, parents, uncles, dear friends—not around to see Kris Bryant make that throw to Anthony Rizzo for the final out. The impromptu sentiments of generations of Cubs fans were genuine and heartfelt. I get goose bumps whenever I think about those messages on the walls.

So, the first shout-out goes to the dedicated Cubs fans—everyone from President Barack Obama's speechwriter to the folks I saw each spring in Mesa, Arizona, to the regulars in the Wrigley Field bleachers (I owe many of them a beer). You inspired me. Thanks for reading.

I covered the Cubs for more than 30 years, the last 18 for MLB.com, and there are many who deserve an assist. My thanks to baseball historian Ed Hartig for his insights and fact-checking. Extra credit goes to the Cubs' media relations staff: Peter Chase, Jason Carr, and Alex Wilcox.

David Ross is the 16th Cubs manager on whom I've reported (and that includes the interim guys) since I started writing from Wrigley Field in 1987. Times have definitely changed from when writers would sit in the dugout before games and listen to Don Zimmer tell stories. All the managers treated me with respect, and I appreciate that.

During my first Cubs spring training, I stayed at the Mezona Hotel in downtown Mesa, Arizona. So did a lot of the young Cubs players, including Shawon Dunston. One day, he approached me at the hotel and wanted to know what it was like being a woman reporter in the clubhouse. I explained how I needed to go in there to get interviews and that I'd learned from the *New York Times'* Jane Gross to approach players as if I were talking to a brother. (When Gross told me that—we were both on assignment in 1981 at old Met Stadium in Minnesota—she was wearing a leather jacket that one of the Yankees players had loaned her because she hadn't come prepared for the frigid press box in domeless Bloomington.)

I thanked Dunston for asking.

I am grateful to the many players I've interviewed over the years (including Dunston's son, Shawon Jr., who was a Cubs draft pick in 2011). I tapped into my personal archives for many of these chapters and cherish the trust and the time players have given me.

When I explained this book to Rizzo and asked him to write the foreword, he said he was hoping to be one of the "moments." It was easy to accommodate the first baseman, who has become the new Mr. Cub.

Finally, I could not have done this book without the support and editing skills of my husband, Alan Solomon. He did lobby for a chapter on his favorite player, George Altman. Maybe next time.

[Sources]

Newspapers and Publications
Chicago Tribune
Cubs *Vine Line*
Los Angeles Times
The Associated Press
The Sporting News

Websites
Baseball-Reference.com
Cubs.com
MLB.com
National Baseball Hall of Fame
Sabr.org/bioproject

Books
Anson, Cap. *A Ballplayer's Career*. CreateSpace Independent Publishing Platform, 2015.

Chicago Tribune staff (edited by Stevenson Swanson). *Chicago Days: 150 Defining Moments in the Life of a Great City*. Cantigny First Division Foundation (produced and distributed by Contemporary Books), 1997.

Devaney, John, and Burt Goldblatt. *The World Series: A Complete Pictorial History*. Rand McNally & Company, 1972.

Durocher, Leo, and Ed Linn. *Nice Guys Finish Last*. University of Chicago Press, 1975.

Kogan, Rick. *A Chicago Tavern: A Goat, a Curse, and the American Dream*. Lake Claremont Press, 2006.

Light, Jonathan Fraser. *The Cultural Encyclopedia of Baseball*. McFarland & Company, 1997.

Muskat, Carrie. *Banks to Sandberg to Grace: Five Decades of Love and Frustration with the Chicago Cubs*. Contemporary Books, 2001.

Muskat, Carrie. *Sammy Sosa*. Mitchell Lane Publishers, 1999.

Santo, Ron. *Ron Santo: For Love of Ivy*. Bonus Books, 1993.

Solomon, Alan. *A Century of Wrigley Field: The Official History of the Friendly Confines*. Major League Baseball and the Chicago Cubs, 2013.

Veeck, Bill. *Veeck as in Wreck*. University of Chicago Press edition, 2001.

Vorwald, Bob. *Cubs Forever: Memories from the Men Who Lived Them*. Triumph Books, 2008.